American Literature
and the Experience of
Vietnam

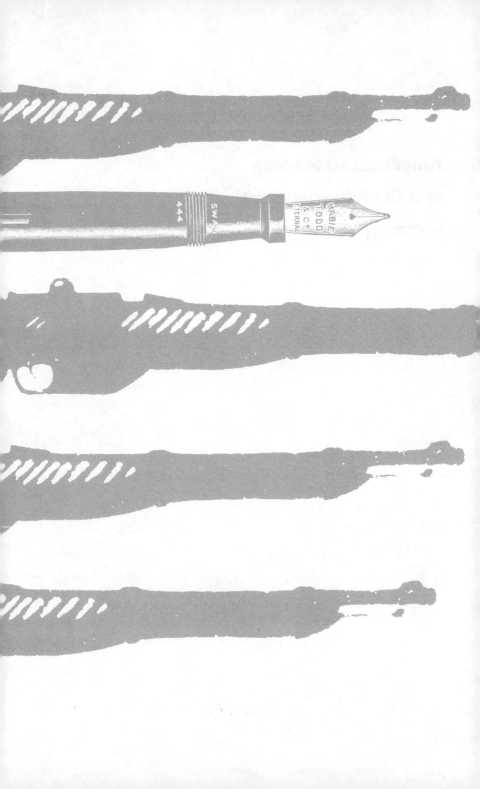

Philip D. Beidler

American Literature and the Experience of Vietnam

The University of Georgia Press   Athens, Georgia

Copyright © 1982 by the University of Georgia Press

Athens, Georgia 30602

All rights reserved

Printed in the United States of America

Designed by Richard Hendel

Set in Trump and Gill Sans

The paper in this book meets the guidelines for
permanence and durability of the Committee on
Production Guidelines for Book Longevity of the
Council on Library Resources.

Library of Congress Cataloging in Publication Data

Beidler, Philip D.
   American literature and the experience of Vietnam.

   1. American literature—20th century—History
and criticism.   2. Vietnamese Conflict, 1961–1975—
Literature and the war.   I. Title.
PS228.V5B4   810'.9'358   81-19845
ISBN 0-8203-0612-6   AACR2

For my mother and father

Contents

Acknowledgments

I would first like to thank the many writers—a good number of them Vietnam veterans—who generously permitted me to discuss their work at length in this study. I would also like to thank a friend and colleague at the University of Alabama, Claudia Johnson, who read much of this in preliminary stages, and who also later, as chairman of the Department of English, got me some research time to put it in final shape. Catherine T. Jones and her staff at the Amelia Gayle Gorgas Library were of enormous help in providing me with various important texts. A leave granted by the university's Office of Academic Affairs in the fall of 1980 allowed me to do most of the writing. Funds were also granted by that office and by the College of Arts and Sciences to help with manuscript preparation. Debbie Davis proved to be a world-class typist. Charles East, of the University of Georgia Press, was an extremely attentive and helpful editor.

In this work, as in all the things I do, I have been sustained by the affection and understanding of Ann McDonald Beidler. I hope it measures up to her intelligence and generosity of spirit.

Grateful acknowledgment is made to those who hold copyright to song lyrics and poems quoted in this volume:
Alkatraz Music Co., for "I Feel Like I'm Fixin' To Die Rag," words and music by Joe McDonald, © 1965/Alkatraz Corner Music 1978, BMI.

Acknowledgments

John Balaban, for *After Our War.*

Earl Barton Music, for "The Letter," recorded by The Box-Tops.

City Lights Books, for "The Teeth Mother Naked At Last," by Robert Bly, © 1970 by Robert Bly.

Frank A. Cross, Jr., for "Rice Will Grow Again."

Michael Cuddihy, for "Monkey," by Bruce Weigl, first published in *Ironwood* VI.

W. D. Ehrhart, for "Vietnam—February 1967."

Stuart Friebert, for "Him, on the Bicycle," by Bruce Weigl, first published in *Field.*

The University of Georgia Press, for *Saigon Cemetery*, by D. C. Berry.

Galway Kinnell, for "Vapor Trail Reflected in the Frog Pond," first published in *Where Is Vietnam?*, Walter Lowenfels, ed.

Perry Oldham, for "War Stories."

Basil T. Paquet, for "Night Dust-Off."

Larry Rottmann, for "The Weather of Vietnam."

Screen Gems-EMI Music Inc./Colgems-EMI Music Inc., for "We Gotta Get Out of This Place," words and music by Barry Mann and Cynthia Weil, © 1965 Screen Gems-EMI Music Inc. Used by permission. All rights reserved.

Robert Shapard, for "Sailing to Bien Hoa," by Bruce Weigl, first published in *Western Humanities Review.*

Dave Smith, for "A Romance," by Bruce Weigl, first published in *The Back Door.*

Bruce Weigl, for *A Romance.*

Yale University Press, for *Obscenities*, by Michael Casey, © 1972 by Yale University Press.

Preface

The title I have chosen for this book is as purposeful as I can make such a thing. It has not been weighed out for its sober heft upon the page or some implication of grave and unavoidable significance. I mean what it says. This book is about the literary ways in which people have tried to talk about an experience called Vietnam—as opposed to a complex of memories, imaginings, and associations called Vietnam, yet most often contemplated mainly in terms of assorted moral or intellectual conceits.

This granted, I mean the book to be a case study in literature and literary consciousness considered in relation to the larger process of cultural myth-making—a study focusing here specifically on one of the most troubled and confusing passages in our history, a sustained collective encounter with our own best and worst selves that came to be the dominant feature of national life in the third quarter of this century. As might be suspected, it also becomes along the way a study of what Paul Fussell has characterized in an analogous context as the curious reciprocity of art and life.[1] To put things more simply, it considers not only how art imitates life but also how, within the evolution of culture, life may also be said frequently to imitate art as well.

Although much of the literature I deal with is about the war itself, I do not mean to suggest in this regard that any final or complete unriddling of the experience of Vietnam will come of it exclusively or even predominantly. Vietnam did not happen only to Americans who went there; neither has the status of participant or firsthand witness seemed to offer any special access to significance. C. D. B. Bryan's *Friendly Fire*, for instance, in its depiction of the anguish and confused rage of an Iowa family over the loss of a son, killed by his own artillery, says some unutterably "true" things about Vietnam as experience that perhaps no other book could possibly say. The "truest" book I know, on the other hand, about what Vietnam was actually like in terms of pure rendering of what Henry James would have called density of "detail," "solidity of specification," "the air of reality,"[2] is Michael Herr's *Dispatches*; but it is still, first and last, the work of an observer, enclosed in its own stoned objectivism like an insect in amber, all the details there, yet fixed in strange, abstract monochrome. In many ways its edgy, disturbing obverse, Gloria Emerson's *Winners and Losers*, eschews any pretense of modulated observation in an attempt to go directly to the experiential heart of things; but precisely as it gets closest to this painful center, it often gets most thoroughly lost in its own anger and polemicism.

In contrast, Norman Mailer's *Why Are We in Vietnam?* quite intentionally never gets to the war at all. Just so, the book unerringly locates Vietnam in at least one primary form of its "reality" as a state of consciousness, a disaster waiting to happen across the whole common range of the national character. Similarly, four major books of poems, Michael Casey's *Obscenities*, D. C. Berry's *Saigon Cemetery*, John Balaban's *After Our War*, and Bruce Weigl's *A Romance*, are all partly "about" Vietnam and partly "about" America, and by being about each are always about the other as well. David Rabe, the most significant American playwright to deal with the war, and Robert Stone, whose novel entitled *Dog Soldiers* likewise "leaves"

Vietnam only to come close to putting all the experience in a single book, seem to suggest that only by bringing the war home in a literal as well as a symbolic sense, locating its reality in the domestic matrix of our collective being, can it be made to signify at all.

Important versions of the war from a closer experiential stance appear in soldier-memoirs such as Tim O'Brien's *If I Die in a Combat Zone,* Philip Caputo's *A Rumor of War,* and Ron Kovic's *Born on the Fourth of July,* and oral histories such as Al Santoli's *Everything We Had* and Mark Baker's *Nam,* as well as in a number of rather traditional novels of combat: David Halberstam's *One Very Hot Day;* Josiah Bunting's *The Lionheads;* Robert Roth's *Sand in the Wind;* William Pelfrey's *The Big V;* Charles Durden's *No Bugles, No Drums;* Larry Heinemann's *Close Quarters;* Winston Groom's *Better Times Than These;* James Webb's *Fields of Fire.* The truth of what happened finds significant literary expression also in works such as Ronald J. Glasser's *365 Days,* Gustav Hasford's *The Short-Timers,* and Charles Coleman's *Sergeant Back Again,* that reduce the experience itself to a kind of brutal, undifferentiated *cinéma vérité,* and equally in others such as William Eastlake's *The Bamboo Bed* and Tim O'Brien's *Going after Cacciato* that carry it all the way over into surreal fantasy.

What the best writing about Vietnam does seem to have in common is a commitment on one hand to an unstinting concreteness—a feel for the way an experience actually seizes upon us, seizes all at once as a thing of the senses, of the emotions, of the intellect, of the spirit—and on the other a distinct awareness of engagement in a primary process of sense-making, of discovering the peculiar ways in which the experience of the war can now be made to signify within the larger evolution of culture as a whole. This is not to say that the writers of Vietnam deny the influence of their literary ancestors. Often they admit to it openly, although like the important writers of most periods they also at times reinvent precisely the images of ancestry they need to define their own uniqueness. Yet here too they testify to an immense awareness of "influence" in the largest sense of that term, of the infinitely diverse ways in which the forms of cultural myth-making often find themselves strangely recapitulated in the content of historical actuality, even as that actuality undergoes the process of becoming itself the basis of new cultural myth.

This task of sense-making would be beset with uncommon challenge. As I will suggest presently, the experience of Vietnam, for those who underwent it, does seem in many ways to have been a thing genuinely peculiar unto itself, a self-contained world, a complete system. Ineluctably theirs, the vision of the war could only by itself, on its own terms, in their memory, begin to signify, and then often in ways that would remain essentially private, or at least self-delimiting in their public effect. Yet as I will also suggest presently it was in perhaps an equal number of ways a phenomenon for which a good portion of our historical or cultural memory at large could serve as a source of symbolic prefiguration. Moreover, there might also eventually be found new possibilities of imaginative invention, new projections of mythic consciousness, so to speak, ways of extending experiential memory into new contexts of collective vision. Ineluctably theirs, the experience of Vietnam would have to become ours both in its very uniqueness and also in the ways that it could ultimately be made, in the dimension of myths past, present, and future, to touch on some sense of our imaginative, and even our spiritual, commonality as a people.

American Literature
and the Experience of
Vietnam

I.

Situation Report: The Experience of Vietnam

I can't say now if I was one of the lucky ones. Sometimes I wish I could've just went ahead and died with my friends. I used to say, "I'm only dreaming. I'll wake up one day. I will wake up." But I never woke up.

Al Santoli, *Everything We Had*

In Nam they called grunts kings. I walked with kings. These people were going to get shit on when they came back here, but in Vietnam they were kings. There was no bullshit. You get in a fire fight and you see exactly who's who. There wasn't anything phony. It was all very real, the realest thing I've ever done. Everything since seems totally superfluous. It's horseshit.

We had a saying about how bad a thing could be: As bad as a day in the Nam.

Mark Baker, *Nam*

Sitrep. Anyone who went to Vietnam or who has had any contact with the military services will recognize the term. Situation Report: a current analysis of a given operation or endeavor. The emphasis is on fluidity, ongoing development, continuing evolution. It proved to be an especially apt expression with regard to the experience of Vietnam: something always going on, something in constant process with little promise or even prospect of significant conclusion. It is noteworthy, for instance, that most American veterans of Vietnam would find two related expressions—"before-action report" and "after-action report"—decidedly less familiar. They were things that they almost never heard except perhaps at the very upper levels of command, where the possibility of a certain abstraction, a sense that things could have a beginning, a middle, and an end was, if nothing else, an encouraging thought.

For most Americans in Vietnam, however, nothing in the war, it seemed, ever really began for any particular reason, and nothing in the war ever really ended, at least as it concerned those still living and unwounded. This is true from that morning, now almost twenty years ago, in the Delta just outside Saigon, when a young U.S. Army Specialist Fourth Class— James T. Davis, age twenty-five, Livingston, Tennessee—became the war's first official American combat fatality, to the moment when the passenger door closed behind the last American advisor on the last plane out of Tan Son Nhut nearly fifteen years later. In the large view or in the small, there was no real beginning and there was no real end to anything having to do with the war. It just went on.

It went on, moreover, for many Americans at least, in a

strange, remote midworld where visitations of the absurd and unreal nestled with sinister ease amidst a spectacle of anguish, violence, and destruction almost too real to be comprehended. Most of the time in Vietnam, there were some things that seemed just too terrible and strange to be true and others that were just too terrible and true to be strange. Indeed, the dominant impression one got of the American experience there, as Michael Herr has written with tense exactitude, was of pure, manic contradiction, of the abiding unreality, in some cases, of that which seemed most real, and of the utter reality, in others, of things so monstrously concrete and immediate that they could only be handled by imaginative conversion into some unreal other. "There were posh fat air-conditioned camps like comfortable middle-class scenes with the violence tacit, 'far away,'" and a short helicopter's flight in the distance there were "places that were so grim they turned to black and white in your head five minutes after you'd gone."[1] Moving within the safe and Stateside-like confines of Bien Hoa Post, one could come across a sign that told more of the story than anyone would ever again need to know: THE ONLY U.S. RIFLE RANGE OCCUPIED BY THE ENEMY DURING THE TET OFFENSIVE. FORTY-EIGHT KILLED DOWNRANGE. AIRBORNE.[2]

This sense of bizarre juxtaposition was not some observer's intellectual conceit. It was as present as the tight, foetid air in which one moved. Base-camp "shoeshine boys and laundresses and honey-dippers," writes Herr, "would starch your fatigues and burn your shit and then go home and mortar your area" (*Dispatches*, p. 14). Meanwhile, their American souls fortified by the ministrations of GI chaplains, "the best-armed patrols in history went out after services to feed smoke to people whose priests could let themselves burn down to consecrated ash on street corners" (p. 45). Airmobile assault companies would lift off from operations where they had come up dry for thirty days and then four kilometers and fifteen minutes away find themselves getting murdered in a hot LZ. Artillery observers from patrols getting blown away by mortars would call for counterstrikes and be denied because they were being shelled from a "friendly" village.

In such a world, to borrow an observation from David Halberstam's *One Very Hot Day*, among the first important novels to come out of the war, one of the most serviceable lessons an American could learn about sanity, and maybe even survival, was that "yes was no longer yes, no was no longer no, maybe was more certainly maybe."[3] So it was in Vietnam with all attempts at signification. To try to talk or write about it, before, during, or after the fact, was to risk being swept up into a self-contained universe of discourse where everything from official euphemism to battlefield slang seemed the product of some insane genius for making reality and unreality—and thus, by implication, sense and nonsense—as indistinguishable as possible. In operations orders, "search and destroy" first became "search and clear," then "reconnaissance in force," and finally "ground reconnaissance." As far as the field manuals and the tactical summaries were concerned, the mission never changed. It was there in black and white: "Find the enemy, engage him, close with him by fire and maneuver, and destroy him." Or, in the more colloquial version fostered by the Eleventh Armored Cavalry, "Find the bastards and pile on." The operations orders were a matter of convenience: the mission was still search and destroy; black simply became white and vice versa. In a similar vein, Michael Herr recalls, at Saigon briefings, dead Vietnamese were "believers" and a decimated American platoon "a black eye" (*Dispatches*, p. 42). As recorded in Charles Durden's *No Bugles, No Drums*, "eight grass huts" could, with mystic ease, become "an enemy base camp," while "two fallen logs across a stream" turned into "an enemy bridge" and "a big pig" into "an enemy pack animal."[4]

None of this really surprised or particularly troubled most American GIs. They were busy making their own mental and metaphorical adjustments. With creative insouciance they baited death, called him names, talked him down. Men did not die. They got "dinged," "waxed," "wasted," "zapped," "snuffed," "greased," "lit up," "blown away." The ever-threatening, elusive enemy took on a series of nicknames, each increasingly chummy. "Victor Charlie" became "Charles," "Chuck," "Old Clyde." Vietnam was written off as a place too incomprehensible to exist. People did not go home. They went "back to the world."

Ironically, if and when they finally did, they often found themselves in the predicament of having to address the same perceptual dilemma all over again, only now with its key terms shifted precisely in reverse. They found, for instance, that the war itself, especially for those who had spent a lot of time in the field, had become as enduringly real to them as the daily rocket attack or the last body they saw going out in a bag. They heard noises in their heads, shouts, hisses, explosions, high-pitched babbling cries of panic and confusion. They heard radio sounds: the feathered, even monotone of the dustoff pilot three minutes out and asking for smoke; the thin, polite jabber of the Aussie spotter pilot bringing in his jets for the strike; the harried, fuzzy squawk of the artillery RTO calling in his contact mission on the deck; or maybe, in the most desperate, bloody hour of the longest day that would ever be, the bright, insipid croon of AFVN Radio Saigon doing time and temperature and cheerily "sending out a little 'Light My Fire' to the headhunters of Bravo Three-Seven."[5] They heard all this, moreover, in the increasing knowledge that they were alone with it. They found that save for other Americans who had been there or had some other direct communication—someone in the family who had managed to come home, or maybe, often enough, someone who hadn't—the actuality of the experience, even for all its years of floating up across the face of the six o'clock news, could not have been harder for most of their countrymen to comprehend or even concern themselves about, especially toward the last, if it had taken place in another galaxy. And for all it mattered, some of the survivors came to think after a while, maybe it actually did.

They had come from the place that was the war, a complete structure of physical and psychic actuality, a whole self-defining system. To begin at any point was to invoke all the rest.

There was time, for instance. It was measured on a single standard, take it or leave it: "in-country." The working unit was the day. The standard tour for Army and Air Force was three hundred sixty five. The Marines, still making a point of their willingness to suffer more and longer than anyone else, did it in months and added one for bad luck: thirteen. Those who cared to count did it in reverse, counted down, rather than up. Most tried not to think about it until the hundred mark, at which point it became nearly impossible to think about much of anything else. Under that it was time to be a "two-digit midget." Later on it was time to be "short"—as in "so short I can't get out of bed in the morning" or "so short that every time I put on my socks I blindfold myself." The best came last: "I'm so short I'm gone."

Then there was space, distance. There was distance back to the world, of course, but for most people that was so incomprehensible that it wasn't worth thinking about. Even airmobile distance was pretty much the same way, something close to a warp in the middle of the universe. What you could cover in a quick ride, coming in or going out, was the equivalent of changing worlds. The only kind of distance a GI could think about really, and stay close to sane, was something that could be related to the next step—one more yard sweated out, no mine, no booby trap, no sniper, no ambush. At the most, the number of steps it took to get down another klick and the number of klicks in one more patrol or sweep.

As in the big categories, so in the small. There wasn't a corner of the experience where the war did not wind up imposing its own self-generated rules. Every grunt knew at least one bunch of refugee huts just outside the wire called "Dogpatch," one firebase called "the Alamo," one provincial town called "Dodge City," one part of the boundary that marked the way to "Indian country." Every outfit had at least one guy named "Shake," good and tough and smart, but jumpy as hell from being on an ambush that got wiped out so long ago that only a few short-timers could remember it. There was always somebody black named "Superfly" and at least one guy, too stoned and crazy to ever get right again, that everybody just called "Space." There was always "Crazy" Somebody-or-Other, usually a machine gunner or a guy with a blooker who could really get with it, loved to bring smoke on anything that moved. If someone thought about it long enough, he could even start to wonder if anybody had a real name any more. Officers: "the old man," "the el-tee," "six," "the actual" (as in, "Let me talk to your 'actual'"). Old-line NCOs, "lifers": "top," "gunny," "mess daddy," "the first shirt." Instant NCOs, fresh from the academy: "Pillsbury," "Shake 'n' Bake," "Ready Whip." The grunts: "Dago," "Ski," "Chief," "Doc," "Red," "Dipstick," "Shortround," "The Professor," "The Sandman" (he makes people

8

sleep). Nobody almost ever had a first name, that was for sure. A man could go through a whole year in Vietnam and never hear anybody called John or William or Bob or Edward (unless maybe it was an officer talking to another officer). What he would remember hearing would be "Jackson" and "Ramos" and "Miller" and "Bell."

There were also other names to remember and speak almost reverently, as if they were some kind of bad magic. "Charlie Alpha"—going in, combat assault. "Lima Zulu"—landing zone. "Cold"—no enemy. "Hot"—a world of hurt. "Dustoff"—going out the bad way, wounded or dead. "Arclight"—B-52s at thirty thousand feet, bringing the max on somebody's ass. "Spooky the Flareship," lighting up the jungle night. "Puff the Magic Dragon," coming up on station and getting ready to unload. Voices in the sky. Names from another world.

Getting a handle on the experience once it was over, then, was not just a question of "readjustment" of the sort imaged in the story they told in every unit about the kid on the first night home at the dinner table who calmly asks his mother to pass the fucking butter or who gets up after the meal, goes outside the back door, and scrapes off his china plate into the garbage can. Rather it was a problem of "vision" in its largest sense—of having undergone an experience so peculiar unto itself and its own insane dynamic as to make nothing in life ever look altogether sane again—and subsequently (and here would be their real point of difference from other veterans of other American wars), of being sentenced, by unspoken national consent, to solitary confinement with the memory of it, urged to tell no tales, please, on the grounds that even were the experience of Vietnam to prove susceptible eventually to certain methods of explanation, there would be virtually no one in the entire country who would care to hear about it.

How, then, might one come up with some form of sense-making for this thing—this experience already cast in the image of some insane metafiction recreating itself in actual life—and in the process find some reason to believe that the effort might be of some literary or cultural significance? There was, of course, the example of *Catch-22*, itself in many ways, or at least so it seemed, an almost perfect formal analogue to the subject at hand. While that might have been true in the abstract, however, in practical terms it came off as too ready-made and prescriptive, too much a kind of available literary conceit far more interesting for its own aesthetic and intellectual possibilities than for the prospect of any large significance it might be made to squeeze out of the experience at hand. For Vietnam *as experience*, even in all its various plenitude of high-grade explosive horror and madness, just couldn't make the grade of cosmic irony required for the metaphorical construct; it just couldn't be pumped up enough to support such an aesthetic occasion. Its Yossarians tended to stay on this side of the water, caught up in various forms of domestic embroilment that even when they got deadly serious were hard to see that way: Jerry Rubin summoning pranksters to the barricades; Abbie Hoffman playing gonzo Paul Revere; Weathermen blowing themselves up by mistake in the basement of their brownstone bomb factory; FBI-league radicals getting themselves caught over a forgotten lid of dope. Likewise, the war came up short on usable villains. The general, Westmoreland, never got beyond seeming mainly just a hapless, well-intentioned Eagle Scout of a soldier assigned to a business that from the start had not been his to make *or* win. And for all the monstrousness of what was wrought at My Lai, the focal participant in that particular horror, Calley, a sorry, insecure punk turned butcher-scapegoat, proved far less than metaphysically compelling in his appointed role as well. There was the Saigon flyboy and his stewardess wife, dark glasses, six-guns, and matching go-to-hell jumpsuits, and at home, the architect of it all, teasing Luci, picking up beagles by the ears, showing off his gall-bladder scar. It was all, finally, just too dismal and botched and banal.

At best, then, *Catch-22*, with its almost sublime spirit of absurd apocalypse, seemed to bear on the attempt to make literary sense of Vietnam only insofar as it suggested something like a set of mathematical upper limits. Indeed, perhaps the most immediate set of formal analogies seemed to offer itself precisely at the opposite end of the aesthetic spectrum, lodged resolutely in the domain of the everyday and quotidian. They were analogies that lay, in a word, in the familiar conventions of television, and, to be more specific, in those associated with the popular, kid-vid version that, by the mid-1960s, could be said to have nurtured the sense-making faculties of at least one whole truly captive American generation—the one, by no coincidence at all, that did most of the fighting and dying in Vietnam.

Golden-age TV: cartoons, commercials, cowboys, comedians and caped crusaders, all coming across together at quantum-level intensity, in a single frantic continuum of noise, color, and light—child-world dreams of aggression and escape mixed up with moralistic fantasies of heroism beleaguered yet ultimately regnant in a world of lurking, omnipresent dangers and deceits—in sum, a composite high-melodrama and low-comedy videotape of the American soul.

Vietnam was all that and more. Just when the spirit of the thing seemed to be straining hardest, however fecklessly, after some grand and sublime seriousness, the matter of the thing was generally well into the process of slopping all the way over into the ludicrous and banal other side; and when things were not happening this way, of course, they were happening in reverse. It *was* in many ways as Norman Mailer, speaking more truth as usual than he knew, had predicted: if the Second World War had turned out to be *Catch-22*, he said, this one was going to have to look more like *Naked Lunch*[6]—an experience not so much apocalyptic in any absolute sense of the term as mainly just loud, violent, crazed, and lurid. He was right. Vietnam was always, in a single moment, dreadful, funny, nightmarish, ecstatic. In its moments of highest drama, it was always its own best and worst parody.

Television especially, among all forms of expression with which we are most currently familiar, had rehearsed this sort of business for a long time. As nearly all of us know from our experience with the medium, for instance, most melodramas are hardly meant to be funny. Often their subject is the depiction of savage, violent adventure, of some radical conflict between the forces of good and the forces of evil, of psychoerotic fantasy, of even outright horror. Yet as we also know, these often turn out to be funny almost beyond belief, their garish, strident exaggeration making them most risible of all precisely in those moments when they purport to be most serious. On the other hand, entertainments, usually in the spirit of the low comic, that are actually meant to be funny—those depicting the domestic struggle of the sexes, for instance, the adventures of humanoid cartoon animals, or the travails of sagacious, popeyed children—may indeed contain much that makes us laugh, but it is more often than not mixed with a good deal of high-grade hideousness: painful accidents and embarrassments, random catastrophes, physical and spiritual torments that often thread only the barest of passages between amusement and outright atrocity.

Now whether at a certain point Vietnam simply started looking like a second-rate *Catch-22* (and later on, *Slaughterhouse Five* and *Gravity's Rainbow*) mixed with some witless version of "concept" TV gotten horribly out of hand, or whether an inescapable process of cultural conditioning had dictated from the outset that it could have hardly turned out to look like anything else, is probably by now something that is just not worth trying to figure out. Like most things connected with the war, it just happened.

It happened everywhere in Vietnam, and it happened all the time. The place became its own bizarre, hermetic mythology. Innocent, bloodied eighteen-year-olds tossed off smooth, ugly, epigrammatic zingers. Michael Herr recalls a classic: Reporter—"How long you been in Vietnam, son?" Infantryman—"All fucking day" (*Dispatches*, p. 179). Ear collectors or not, members of ambush patrols could chuckle up a little bravado late at night remembering the story everyone heard at least once about "the guy up north" who was "building his own gook." True or not, it was an article of common faith that George Patton's son, a regimental commander of armored cavalry, had once gotten up Christmas cards picturing a mound of enemy corpses and bearing the legend "Peace On Earth."[7] There was for sure a Green Beret officer in I Corps who wore an extra dog tag that read, "If you are recovering my body, fuck you."[8] Any battle plan involving the tactical use of napalm automatically came to be called "Operation Crispy Critter." In a macabre variation on the same theme, there seems to have been at least one occasion, according to the memoirs of a young lieutenant of marines, in which pigs were witnessed after a battle contentedly eating the flesh of roast people.[9]

In the midst of all this, Americans in Vietnam looked for something, anything, to sustain the flow of psychic energy that finally had to substitute altogether for even the most remote

sense of purpose. Stoned out of their skulls, weighed down
with their totems, their talismanic nicknames and buddy-lore,
their freaky bravado, Jim Morrison and Janis Joplin and Jimi
Hendrix and the Stones blasting away in their ears, they carried
the fight until they got hurt or killed or just until their time
was up and they got to go home.

Home. The land of the big radio, across the ocean a gigan-
tic set of speakers at max volume. The songs were the same
everywhere:

> We gotta get out of this place,
> If it's the last thing we ever do.
>
> Gimme a ticket for an air-o-plane,
> Ain't got time to take a fay-ust train,
> Lonely days are gone,
> I'm agoin' home,
> My baby done sent me a letter.

The only difference between them and Monterrey Pop or Alta-
mont was the guns, and maybe, in a squared-away unit, the
haircuts.

"Born to be wild." They were always there, in every unit,
usually sad, dufus little guys, trying to get the message out to
somebody by blazoning it as big as they could. America's best,
born in the image of the mean, funky gods they had come
to worship, acting out the drama for real, the killers on the
road. "Get some, snake," they muttered righteously, as Cobra
gunships streaked across a treeline, dealing beautiful death.
"Willie Peter, make you a buh-liever," they chanted with delir-
ious joy as artillery came crashing in on call. "The 'Nam Can
Kill Me, But It Can't Make Me Care,"[10] they bragged on their

flak jackets and helmet covers from the DMZ to the Delta. It became the cry of their defiance. But still always after all the noise and light and motion, there came back more than anything else just the silent, suffocating truth that it was surely enough the biggest game there was: cowboys versus gooks, played in every moment for terrible stakes, and for reasons that no one would ever be able to explain.

Audace! Audace! Toujour l'audace!

Gung Ho! Gung Ho! Gung Ho! Pray for war!

Some old sense of high drama born of a national dream of heroism now interfused itself again and again with a bad case of sophomoric hardass. Americans went on calling the enemy "the bad guys" and friendly troops "the little people" and tagging the whole bunch as much as possible in terms of generic caricatures—dinks, slants, slopes, gooks, zips—because only in this way could they handle their befuddlement and irritation at nearly everything they had to do. They simply could not understand the stolidity, the caution, the patience, the quiet capacity to endure and little else of the people whose geopolitical rights they were supposedly protecting. Neither could they come to grips with the sullen tenacity and faith of modern ideological warriors, foes who had been fighting the war long before many of their American opposite numbers had been born. To compound matters, even as GIs and marines went on killing Asians, they also went on fighting each other in varying misbegotten combinations—draftees versus lifers; field soldiers versus housecats and poges and sundry other REMF (rear-echelon-motherfucker) sons of bitches; white beneficiaries of post–World War II peace and plenitude versus blacks evincing a profound spiritual reluctance to fight what seemed in too many ways a racist war waged by a racist army in a land of people whose condition they perceived as greatly analogous to their own at home.

As they used to say in Vietnam, "There it is." It was the only comment possible at the time, and it perhaps still comprehends much of what one can say even in retrospect. We are only just now beginning to learn to make it signify. One names the old names, and only in the barest terms does it allow itself to come together. Khe Sanh is still mainly just a place defended for a while at great bloody cost and then abandoned again to the elements and an occasional enemy patrol. Tet remains not so much a battle as whatever firefight one happened to get into that day and in the days that followed until the war eventually tailed off again into much the same old deadly stalemate as before. The only people who remember much about the Ia Drang, the A Shau, Hamburger Hill, the Ho Bo Woods, the Pineapple Plantation, Xuan Loc, Lai Khe, Quan Loi, Dau Tieng, the Old French Fort, and all the other names and places were those who had actually gone there and spilled the blood and the anger and the youth.

Mainly, Vietnam would always be a place with no real points of reference, then *or* now. As once in experiential fact, so now in memory as well. It would become the task of the Vietnam writer to create a landscape that never was, one might say—a landscape of consciousness where it might be possible to accommodate experience remembered within a new kind of imaginative cartography endowing it with large configurings of value and signification. In this way, what facts that could be found might still be made to mean, as they had never done by themselves, through the shaping, and ultimately the transforming power of art.

2.

American Literature:
Prophecy and Context

"There are good wars and bad wars," Lieutenant Hamilton said, looking clean and bright and sure of himself. "I want my war to be a good one."

Daniel Ford, *Incident at Muc Wa*

You couldn't find two people who agree about when it began, how could you say when it began going off? Mission intellectuals like 1954 as the reference date; if you saw as far back as War II and the Japanese occupation you were practically a historical visionary. "Realists" said that it began for us in 1961, and the common run of Mission flack insisted on 1965, post–Tonkin Resolution, as though all the killing that had gone before wasn't really war. Anyway, you couldn't use standard methods to date the doom; might just as well lay it on the proto-Gringos who found the New England woods too raw and empty for their peace and filled them up with their own imported devils.

Michael Herr, *Dispatches*

American writing about Vietnam, for all one's sense of the new and even unprecedented character of the experience it describes, often turns out to be very much in context, so to speak, with regard to our national traditions of literature and popular myth-making at large. As with so many other features of our history and culture, it seems almost as if our classic inheritance of native expression has prophesied much of what we now know of Vietnam, made it by self-engendering symbolic fiat part of our collective mythology long before it existed in fact.

One thinks of the war planners at MACV Saigon scheming away in command centers as secure from the impingements of human reality as their own hermetic certitude and remembers Ahab pondering his lines and charts yet all the while knowing these to have been superseded by some inner calculus that is the function of his own fine monomania. In the same prophetic connection, one thinks about the U.S. mission with all its romantic adventurers and apostles of enlightened value (their image frozen once and for all in the snapshot that would haunt its subject into changing the course of history: Daniel Ellsberg, apprentice spook in his rakish paramilitary fatigues, the Harvard boy knee-deep in the elephant grass, his forearm cradling a Swedish K) and remembers Ishmael and his combination of incorrigible comic innocence and "genial desperado" effrontery. For all his essential acuteness of perception and his unspoiled, saving humor, the best thing in him, he can still talk warmly about being "social" with "a horror." The imagination simply balks at the idea of such a line in the mouth of Conrad's Marlow or Kurtz, or at the possibility of either, through some strange democratic avidity of the heart, conceiving of a savage companion as "George Washington cannibalistically developed."[1] Other prophetic images abound. There is Cooper's Natty Bumppo (or perhaps, more properly, what we have since made of him), the hard-eyed ascetic, erstwhile saint and full-time gunman, the democratic stalwart cum eternal irregular warrior. He is both the prophet of westward-hastening empire and its kept outrider. He is, like his successors in Vietnam, grandly, even sublimely oblivious to the damning irony of a view of culture that can somehow divide the rest of the world into "good" Indians (those who can turn out to be just like us) and "bad" ones (those who cannot), that defines the earthly mission of that culture in terms of propagating in the name of good the implicit, self-feeding racism that is its special hidden curse. Similarly prophetic, in a world where good and bad Indians are often hard to tell apart, is the reduction of the idea of moral manhood into what, for all the hero's protestations of commitment to rather conventional standards of truth and humane value, is essentially a self-isolating pride in one's capacity for survival and ever-reliable ability to deal death.

There is Melville's Starry Vere, the courageous, self-reliant leader fated by what he takes to be the force of immediate historical circumstance and the claims of patriotic and military responsibility to see through to its wrong, shabby, sorrowful end a tragedy of misperception and needless sacrifice. Billy Budd, for all the goodness and beauty in him (and this despite the fatal defect, the curse of his doomed innocence, that causes him in moments of confusion and affront to explode forth in sudden, inexplicable violence), has simply not been with the program; in a world of war, his deadly assault on the master-at-arms Claggart, however justified in terms of some absolute standard of value, is simply an unfortunate incident, a matter to be handled with firmness and expediency. It has had to be judged strictly within the situational context of the mission, and the order of the mission has had to be preserved. It is finally the only way, Vere is convinced, of making the best of an ugly business that he knows somehow to have been wrong from the start.

There is Twain's Hank Morgan, genial tinkerer-technocrat *and* budding Yankee despot. He is the ultimate advisor, the one-man assistance command. With barely disguised condescension, he serves his maddeningly backward and complacent Arthurian hosts, all the while feeding what he eventually discovers to be his own misbegotten dreams of power and mastery. He clears away piece by piece a whole inherited socioreligious order in the name of progress, only to find that he has created the most fertile of open grounds for the nurturing of old quarrels and antagonisms and outright hatreds that he cannot understand in the least. Appropriately, he is at last undone by the awesome plenitude of his own technopolitical inventiveness. (He is, by almost inconceivable prophetic irony, a foreman for the Colt Firearms Company, later the principal contractor in Vietnam for the ill-starred M-16 rifle). Of the many ways he does himself in, along with his last loyal minions, the one that quite literally gets him in the end is his ability to find almost infinitely new ways for dealing out destruction and death. Here will be no last, long-shot helicopter lifting off from the embassy roof. He is at the last his own best victim.

In the broadest symbolic terms, finally, one can also look back even to the earliest reports of exploration and settlement and conquest from our colonial diarists and historians and sense that the experience of Vietnam is in certain uncanny ways already there—already there, perhaps, 350 years down a dim, beckoning path of discovery and sacrifice and bloodshed and terror—but still there and getting ready from the start to happen inevitably as it would in the end. To this degree Cotton Mather's vision is irrevocably of a piece with Jim Morrison's, John Smith's of a piece with Michael Herr's. Vietnam is prefigured indelibly in the English, Dutch, Spanish, French accounts (not to mention their fictive re-creations by Brockden Brown, Fenimore Cooper, Nathaniel Hawthorne, and a host of others) of the dark woods, the swamps, the mountains, the rivers, the "howling wilderness," to use a recurrent early characterization, tangled, forbidding, dense with all its snares and labyrinthine byways and alive with all the rank power and abundance of original creation. And the experience of the war similarly and equally has its prophecy there in the gliding, shadowed forms of an unseen enemy, the wily inscrutable foe, the specters of the forest, the multitudinous host born of a whole Western world's own best demonological imaginings.

What can be said, of course, about prophecy and prophetic context with regard to Vietnam and our classic literature and cultural myth-making can also be suggested in relation to much of more modern American expression and popular lore as well. If this war in the place called "beyond,"[2] with its flittering, wraithlike terrors, and its sudden explodings-forth into nightmare and pain and waste, truly belonged by way of strange mythic prefiguration to a whole line of classic American isolatos, messiahs, doomed eirons, and sainted ascetic killers, it also belonged equally, and in the same fashion, to a host of movie and TV gunfighters, brave and persevering dogfaces and GI Joes, comic-book champions of truth and right, secret agents and howling commandos and various other enforcers without portfolio. As much as anything else, Vietnam would also turn out to be, as Ward Just observed, "Gary Cooper on the Street Without Joy,"[3] or perhaps, as Michael Herr would later have it, Batman in the Iron Triangle (*Dispatches*, p. 57). Even as the war got on with the long, dismal business of happening in fact, it would still belong for a good while to John Wayne and *his* Green Berets—no matter, as the narrator tells us in Gustav Hasford's *The Short-Timers*, if that meant making movies where the sun, with about as much relation to reality as anything else in the film, is forced to set eastward into the South China Sea (p. 32).

Indeed, how surprised finally could one be about things like this in a world where myth of all manner—old and new, large and small, grand and ephemeral, projection of culture-image born in some cases of the American soul and in others of the American marketplace—seemed persistently bent on affixing itself to reality and refashioning it in shapes of strange, hybrid mutation? Often, it seemed, the stranger the better. Often, the more bizarre or unexpected the coupling, the more surely one felt the sense of confronting the genuine experienced thing, of standing face to face with Vietnam in its full capacity to make an insanity seem somehow strangely normal or a horror somehow strangely incidental and even innocent.

How surprised could one be when the whole apparatus of mythic consciousness seemed to have gone on permanent short-circuit, pure overload? The popular name, as mentioned earlier, for any operation involving napalm—"Crispy Critter"—turned out to be a theft from commercials for a children's breakfast cereal, crackling and sugar-coated, especially popular with the Saturday-morning TV crowd. A death-spewing juggernaut of an aircraft, basically a gun platform with propellers, got *its* name—"Puff the Magic Dragon"—from a soft-core fantasy about happy innocence and love (as well as an endorsement, most people suspected, of smoking marijuana) made famous by a trio of antiwar folksingers. The primary American infantry weapon on the battlefield actually *looked* like a toy and proved appropriately susceptible to breakage and malfunction. ("Made by Mattel, It's Swell," its users would invariably say, after its inevitable misfires, if they had managed to stay alive in the process.)

The war itself would do well enough, of course, at creating in equally manic proportion what seemed an altogether original master iconography, an iconography wholly born, it seemed, of some pure principle of crazed spontaneous self-generation: in Ronald J. Glasser's *365 Days*, field medics pressing a placebo-sacrament of M&M candies to the lips of dying boys, lately come from a childhood of chocolate-factory ads between cartoons, but now with bodies too broken for morphine (p. 54); in Charles Durden's *No Bugles, No Drums*, a young infantryman, driven to madness by a war as "fucked up," he says, "as a picnic in a free-fire zone," searching his base camp for an entire day to find a place to "cover his shit" in literal imitation of superiors who take maximum casualties and accept minimum responsibility (pp. 1, 200); in Larry Heinemann's *Close Quarters*, a trooper looking on in transfixed silence as his best friend turns on a Viet Cong corpse and methodically, industriously, swinging in labored, metronomic cadence a captured AK-47 butt down, like someone chopping wood or beating a rug, reduces the body to an unrecognizable mush;[4] in Tim O'Brien's *Going after Cacciato*, Frenchie Tucker, shot through the nose as he pokes his head into one last tunnel, and Bernie Lynn, who goes in after him, dying of his tunnel wound, straight down into his guts, and Buff, upended "like a praying Arab in Mecca," face down in the muck, his shot-away face sloshing around in his upturned helmet, filling it up with all the life after death there would ever be;[5] in William Pelfrey's *The Big V*, the message left behind by "the Anachronism" after he gets blown away, one valedictory piece of wiseass rebellion from the college boy too far from America to get back, out of place, out of time—"I also wish to be buried face down, but I am sure I won't be. The whole world can still kiss my ass, though."[6]

Yet even as emergent primary images such as these seem to move the literature of Vietnam toward some compelling new architecture of vision uniquely its own, they also recall that sense of grand and enduring mythic centrality often associated with so much of our classic tradition as well. For all their terrible, urgent strangeness, they also possess an older, almost ritualized quality of iconographic permanence. Indeed, it is often precisely the dramatic character of revelatory insight that makes Vietnam writing seem so genuinely unprecedented and novel that in the same moment makes it seem also most paradoxically of a piece with its prophetic context. In passages such as the ones described, we read forward into new possibilities of meaning. Yet at the same time we also read instructively backward after a fashion. We remember the recurrent nightmare of Yossarian's witness to the moment in which Snowden spills his dirty secret of mortality. We recall Henry Fleming's discovery, in his furthest flight from the battlefield's hot horror, of the corpse lodged even at nature's green cathedral heart. And we look afield and beyond to any number of other similar moments of visionary apocalypse that have made our literature so often seem something like an endless series of harrowed exercises in confronting our own passion for extremity. Here, in the literature of our most recent war, is also the most recent of major American cases in which experiential memory, even as it projects itself forward into new forms of imaginative invention that seem to challenge traditional modes of mythic understanding, proves often in retrospect to have shaped itself greatly in their prophetic image as well.

It has generally been Vietnam literature written in a dimension of consciousness where a complex awareness of this process has been not only apparent, but often even a central thematic preoccupation, that has established itself as the most important to come out of the war. Precisely in this quality of visionary openness, this sense of ever-evolving relationship between literary creation and the process of cultural mythmaking at large, it has told about an experience more "real," finally, than any one that ever existed in fact. This is true of all the literature of the war that promises to be of enduring significance: of dramas such as Arthur Kopit's *Indians* and David Rabe's *The Basic Training of Pavlo Hummel, Sticks and Bones,* and *Streamers;* of works of documentary and analysis such as Ward Just's *To What End,* Frances Fitzgerald's *Fire in the Lake,* C. D. B. Bryan's *Friendly Fire,* Gloria Emerson's *Winners and Losers,* and Michael Herr's *Dispatches;* of oral histories such as Al Santoli's *Everything We Had* and Mark Baker's *Nam;* of memoirs such as Tim O'Brien's *If I Die in a Combat Zone,* Philip Caputo's *A Rumor of War,* and Ron Kovic's *Born on the Fourth of July;* of novels such as Norman Mailer's *Why Are We in Vietnam?,* David Halberstam's *One Very Hot Day,* William Eastlake's *The Bamboo Bed,* Josiah Bunting's *The Lionheads,* Robert Roth's *Sand in the Wind,* James Crumley's *One to Count Cadence,* William Pelfrey's *The Big V,* Charles Durden's *No Bugles, No Drums,* Larry

Heinemann's *Close Quarters*, Winston Groom's *Better Times Than These*, James Webb's *Fields of Fire*, Gustav Hasford's *The Short-Timers*, Tim O'Brien's *Going after Cacciato*, and Charles Coleman's *Sergeant Back Again*; of collections of short narrative such as Ronald J. Glasser's *365 Days* and Tom Mayer's *Weary Falcon*; of books of poems such as Michael Casey's *Obscenities*, D. C. Berry's *Saigon Cemetery*, John Balaban's *After Our War*, and Bruce Weigl's *A Romance*. Works such as these locate the experience of Vietnam in its mythic context and acknowledge the shaping power of that context in life and art alike, even as they project their vision of that experience forward imaginatively into a new architecture of mythic consciousness that must be created as its consequence, an architecture of consciousness that will in turn have much to do with the shape and character of actual experience to come.

It is precisely in this sense that Paul Fussell begins *The Great War and Modern Memory* with the assertion that the "real" World War I as most of our century would see it—that singular occurrence he rightly and eloquently describes as the determinant of so much we have come to associate with the sensibility we call "modern" or "ironic"[7]—was surely as much a function, before, during, and after, of collective mythic imagining as it was of any "experience" of the battlefield where it happened in fact. "At the same time the war was relying on inherited myth," he writes, "it was generating new myth, and that myth is part of the fiber of our lives." That is what Fussell means by memory, the degree to which "the dynamics and iconography" of a war turn out to be "crucial political, rhetorical, and artistic determinants of subsequent life."[8] Or, to put it more simply, he reminds us that much we take to be "real" is so, in fact, only as it may be equally considered a function of the various ways we both inherit and invent for mythologizing ourselves in any given moment of our common existence. What Fussell means by memory, then, is akin to what we must understand here with regard to the idea of literary vision as at once both prophecy and context. It is a ground or matrix within which experience appears in significant ways to create itself as the recapitulation of some past symbology founded on a whole inheritance of collective assumption, yet in the same moment generates a new symbology crucial not only to its own apprehension but also to the apprehension of what will pass for "experience" or "reality" in times to come. Here the important American writers of Vietnam find their essential domain.

3.

Early Vietnam Writing,
1958–1970

When I asked him to what part of the body he hit the man, he
smirked and fixed me with his unblinking eyes and said, "Blew the
fucker's head off. Turned it to jelly." . . .

Steve says the reason the South Vietnamese have such a lousy
army is because everybody's all the time goosing each other.

Martin Russ, *Happy Hunting Ground*

They laid the bodies out in front of the spotting tower and everyone had to come see them, to gape at the guts hanging out of
the one like an atrophied paper-mache leg, to slap me on the
shoulder, to point out my brilliant shooting. It wasn't unlike a
successful hunt, back in camp with the drunk card players who
only hunted peace from their pinched-face Texas wives, middle-
aged men with fawning mouths and bitter, envious eyes, and
hands that grasped at your youth.

James Crumley, *One to Count Cadence*

The preceding epigraphs, from two important early books about Vietnam,[1] reveal that even as the war was still charting out the course of its own grim enactment, it had already come to be imaged in literature pretty much as it would always be: a mixup of American mythic consciousness and realized experiential fact so dense and entangled that from the very beginning there would never be any real hope of sorting it out. Accordingly, the literary interpreters who most often got Vietnam right from the outset began with the premise (or quickly accepted it along the way) that all the basic categories of meaning one might think of—facts and fictions, realities and imaginings, things remembered and things reconstituted in the shapes of collective myth—had to be reckoned in this case as simply and flatly interchangeable.

It was this realization that could make it possible for a book such as William Crawford Woods's *The Killing Zone*[2] to go significantly to the heart of the experience of Vietnam without being literally "about" the war at all. Such is the lesson suggested, for instance, in the novel's last scene. An aging first sergeant, the professional soldier out of date, writes condolence letters to the families of dead draftees. They have been killed as the result of a training accident in a computerized field problem, the brainchild of an overeducated, underexperienced company commander. Through a foul-up in the computer program (a failure to compensate for "memory," to be exact), the machine has been allowed to order live ammunition.

As the sergeant writes, his memory turning in particular to a young NCO protégé who has also died in the incident, died in a ghastly war-game parody of the bayonet drill that has so often been the object for the younger man of a perverse, almost obsessive delight, he finds himself increasingly distracted by music playing too loudly in the background. It is the Stones, doing "Ruby Tuesday." Although he hates nearly everything about "the new music," he has heard this before and liked it, "this quiet tune." It is, he thinks, "a really beautiful song" (p. 179).

In the passage, one can trace out some of the large patterns in what would eventually become familiar as a kind of master iconography of the war. Throughout, Vietnam would be a creation of experts, of planners, of programmers, designers and interpreters of packaged death on printouts, flow charts, overlays, graphs, grand collocations of statistics, with the crucial screwup factor hidden somewhere neatly below the bottom line. New professionals, boy officers with college and graduate-school ideas would make a mess of the war; old professionals, career sergeants on their second and third times through, would forswear any possibility of fixing it up. Meanwhile, draftees, mainly, would do the dying, find *their* bottom line on the battlefield and in the turgid, empty catch-phrases of next-of-kin letters—"It is with deep regret . . . as your husband's commanding officer . . . a good soldier whose loss will be deeply felt" (p. 179). Even the background music is right, although the old sergeant somewhat stumbles across his own point and then misses a good part of it. He gets the appropriate group, if not the tune. Most of the music, unlike his song, would not be pretty. It would come through in the street-fighting lines of "Satisfaction," "Red Rooster," "Sympathy for the Devil."

Conversely, as demonstrated by other early works such as David Halberstam's *One Very Hot Day*, a novel of the war in many ways unsurpassed even until now in its sense of experiential immediacy, it was apparent from the beginning that any book truly "about" Vietnam would also have to be "about" an

America considered in terms of a whole nexus of recurrent mythic symbologies. On the first page, there it all was, the Alamo west—the old seminary, its priests now "all gone back to Europe," encircled with "miles and miles of barbed wire" and "mountains of sandbags." "By the gate," there stands the welcome sign of an American army advisory group ("The Best There Is") and "a caricature of an American officer with a huge grin, and then the initials WETSU"—"We Eat This Shit Up" (p. 1).

It is the last outpost of westward mission, the farthest reach of the word primeval democratic. Big William Redfern, the laughing black ranger captain, leads his charges in its master incantations: "'Good morning, Vienamese,' he would say, then they would answer in a chant he taught them, 'Good morning, Big William.' 'How they hanging, Vienamese?' he would ask and they would answer, their voices thin like school children, 'They hanging fine, Big William'" (p. 12). There was the mission, all right. They did not know how to talk because they had not been to Ranger School at Fort Benning. They did not know how to walk, William's friend Beaupre notes with bemusement, probably because they had not seen enough western movies (p. 26). These things and others they would have to learn.

Thus, recurrently, early Vietnam writing bespoke a sense of the basic interchangeability of life and art, of felt experience and shared imaginative assumption. The "real" Vietnam would often seem so outrageous a piece of artifice—and not the artifice of Samuel Beckett or Jorge Luis Borges or Joseph Heller, but rather that considerably more banal version of cartoons, comic strips, and cut-rate melodrama—that it could only be a creation of "the books"; and equally often, through the assumption of a view born in the idea of calculated artificiality, one could cut down to the very core of the real. This was the most important discovery made by major early writers about Vietnam, and it is the one that has dominated the literature of the war ever since: that what sense was to be made of it at all would lie in the self-conscious exploration of relationships between experiential and aesthetic (and in a vast number of cases, mock-aesthetic) possibilities of truth-telling, in the realization that far from being incompatible or opposite, they would often imply and even entail each other.

It is through a sense of this creative mutuality (largely intuitive in the first case and most grandiosely calculated in the second), for instance, that the two most visible and perhaps even notorious of the "big" early books about the war—Robin Moore's *The Green Berets* and Norman Mailer's *Why Are We in Vietnam?*[3]—turn out ironically, each in its fashion, to have gotten Vietnam right in large measure by going at it in what may have seemed at the time to be all the wrong ways. The first, through the dogged, banal, almost oppressive sincerity of its literalness, arrives at an arrestingly "literary" version of the truth; the second, eschewing from the outset anything but a "literary" address to the question imaged in its title, often comes as close to evoking the literal character of the war as many books that approach it head-on. In variations on these reflexive processes and strategies, a primary mode of Vietnam writing would emerge, a mode that would come to be dominant not only in prose narrative—documentary, memoir, short story, novel—but also in drama and poetry as well.

The two books in question are somewhat curious mirror images of each other. The first is a documentary potboiler, ostensibly conceived of as a popular, adulatory, and above all truthful account of a new breed of soldier in a new kind of war. The second is an unabashedly literary tour de force, proceeding almost exclusively by calculated aesthetic indirection, the work of a writer who is on record as thinking the very idea of a factual account of anything a sublimely irrelevant concern. Yet both texts arrive at remarkably similar visions of what will persist as some central truths of the war.

For all its steamy amateurishness, Moore's book comes off especially now as a remarkable, albeit unconscious exercise in fictive concision and point, its assemblage of documentary vignettes indeed telling with tense, even strained precision, just about all the truth about Vietnam, experiential *and* imaginative, that anyone was ever going to need. It prophesied with innocent exactitude the vision of "the new legions,"[4] to use Donald Duncan's telling phrase, marked out in its depiction of the first wave of Americans to Vietnam the essential character of the strange generation of true *enfants de guerre* who would follow, the "mix" that Michael Herr would later characterize as "incipient saints and realized homicidals, unconscious lyric poets and mean dumb motherfuckers with their brains all down in their necks" (p. 30). In attempting to accredit a contemporary warrior mythos, Moore would also wind up exposing it as a source of savage, surreal grotesquerie. His Vietnam would turn out to be a combination of cartoon-character super-heroism with some nasty little drama of the absurd, country-wide guerrilla theater with live ammunition, a new revelation in strange foreign places of an old, familiar, eternally innocent brand of righteous American overreaching, at once as wondrous and horrific as it always had been before.

That would be Mailer's ultimate revelation as well, although he would arrive at it in somewhat reverse method, through a careening, scabrous, spaced-out parody of precisely the American warrior mythos Moore was trying to exalt. Addressing by aesthetic subterfuge a war he intentionally does not mention until the book's last page, he suggests that for a "true" Vietnam in all its dread bounty of misguided idealism become hard-eyed horror, one need not look beyond the domestic precincts of the national spirit. This wilderness of the soul, a combination of modern wasteland and primal terra incognita, he depicts through the postulation of a symbolic geography encompassing the urban ghetto, the gilded elysium of oil-baron Texas, and the immense silent reaches of Alaska. He describes it all, moreover, in an argot creating its own barbaric poetry of obscene jive and blather, a media rush coming across at once on all possible channels. His point about Vietnam, emerging from the composite spectacle and blare, at the last a kind of garish macho apocalypse intertwined with the lingering stuff of domestic melodrama, turns out to be remarkably similar to that emerging, if somewhat unconsciously, from *The Green Berets*. The people who give us Vietnam, Mailer seems to say (paralleling the observation of an esteemed contemporary, H. Rap Brown), are American naturals, their capacity for violence as innate as their dewy-eyed fondness for cherry pie. Again, as Michael Herr would make clear, this too was the stuff of prophecy and more, the "intro-bleep" (to use one of Mailer's favorite chapter headings) for a "Mission" comparable more than any way else to "a big intertwined ball of baby milk snakes," almost "that innocent, and about that conscious" (p. 44).

The Green Berets would arrive at a similar point, and also like Mailer's book, along the way it would bring to the reader's attention some primary features of what would turn out to be its own curiously original and suggestive brand of literary artifice. Indeed, imaging the reflexive, self-conscious character of both works, Moore's narrative in its first pages supplies a kind of keynote to many early attempts to deal with Vietnam as a literary topic: the initial focus of concern is not with the war as subject but instead with identifying in generic terms the appropriate manner of its depiction. From the outset, however intuitively, this first "big" book about Vietnam focuses itself on the nature of literary process, the idea of sense-making itself. Should the narrative be seen as basic reportage, shaped, edited, infused with color and point, perhaps, but still essentially "factual"? Or might it be best described in terms of one of the more familiar categories of the "creative"—a novel, a collection of stories, a linked series of dramatic vignettes? Moore opts for the latter, calling his work a novel even as he continues to attest to its wholesale veracity. He suggests in this case that fiction will somehow be truer than fact.

Appropriately, from its first episodic chapter onward, Moore's "novel" *and* "book of truth" (p. 11), even as it launches itself on the attempt to get Vietnam right, becomes an inventory of nearly everything that was wrong about the war from beginning to end. At the bottom of the whole business, for instance, there is the problem of Southeast Asia and particularly Vietnam itself. With or without his countrymen, to Moore, in his clear American eyes, it is a morass of corruption, incompetence, and intrigue. Politics and payoffs frequently obscure the dividing lines between friend and enemy, with Asian foes and allies alike seemingly bent more often than not on undoing the work of diligent Americans.

In contrast to the GI stalwarts of the text, for example, the South Vietnamese commanders depicted are almost uniformly venal, cowardly, and self-serving. Given a mission of any danger, they find some excuse to remain within the safe confines of base camp and send out a subordinate in their stead. When they do venture out, they generally succeed in turning routine missions into disasters. Every so often, perhaps, there is a good one, usually of somewhat low rank, not senior enough to get in on the heavy corruption. Usually, at a certain point he will elicit from an American some comment like, "Trung here, though, he's a tiger. If I had a thousand like him, I could win the war in three weeks."

In general, however, this is left to the Green Berets themselves, each of whom frequently seems quite capable indeed of doing it in his own right. If there is much of Natty Bumppo or Jim Bowie about them, though, there is a good deal of James Bond as well. Often, they are foreign nationals—French, German, Czech, Finn—and given the chance they act the role of cosmopolitan savant. They are true connoisseurs—of food, drink, women, weapons, wars, death. To dispel, however, the idea of some mercenary army-within-the-army, Moore is at pains to note the enlistment among their ranks of many eager young West Pointers, heedless of the advice of service traditionalists that such unconventional duty will imperil their careers. Finally, however, no matter what their background or ambitions, most of the Green Berets depicted come off as being at heart resolutely domestic, fighting gamely, expertly, winning their war chiefly that they may return to wife and children and happy home.

To do this, they frequently seem to employ a near-infallible intuition about the enemy and where, when, and how he will strike. They know all his tricks, so to speak, many of them unspeakably dirty, and have learned of necessity ways to beat him at his own nasty game. Trick for trick, trump for trump, they conduct a mirror-image war. A young woman is recruited to seduce a Viet Cong colonel by being shown pictures of pigs feeding on the entrails of her father, a village chief, and her twelve-year-old brother, after they have been disemboweled by an enemy assassination squad (pp. 120–21). A prison full of jail-birds—"Saigon's finest second-story men," one Beret chortles gleefully (p. 145)—is enlisted to snatch the colonel flagrante delicto. A class of ranger candidates led by a cowardly Vietnamese major are used as bait in an ambush designed to trap a French adventurer who leads a crack battalion of VC and specializes in executing Americans (p. 161).

Often, winning the war for the Green Berets also involves the expert use of legerdemain available only through the wonders of American technology, wonders designed to zap Charlie or anyone else when he least expects it. There are hidden Flash Gordon control panels full of mysterious toggle switches, masterpieces of demolition circuitry, their existence revealed usually just at the last moment, just when things seem most desperate. Throw one switch and a hidden row of Claymore mines annihilates an entire wave of attacking enemy; throw another and a turncoat machine-gun crew, raking a camp from the inside, is blown to smithereens by explosives concealed in the sandbagged floor of their position (pp. 67–68).

In *The Green Berets* it is all very much, as Bernard Fall described it, a "Batman" war,[5] with the enemy and all others who impede the cause of right getting zapped generally through a combination of American indomitableness and their own greed, lust, cowardice, opportunism, or plain stupidity. It is fought against all who get in the way of the cause: the VC; the incompetent, corrupt South Vietnamese; the traditionalists of the "straight-leg" conventional army; the Saigon Dial-soapers and paper merchants.

To the credit of Moore's candor, the war is also for a great majority of the time in *The Green Berets* an undeniably dirty business. But in the same moment, it still somehow always manages—even, for instance, as a good and brave American lies dying in the middle of the Asian night with the back of his head blown off—to seem at bottom profoundly unreal, or even worse, not altogether serious. There is always something of the comic-book-cartoon-superhero fantasy about it. There is always something being pulled off or put over on somebody. There is the trick that lures smug VC suspects into a building about to be blown in a fake "mortar attack" (pp. 109–10); there is the con that brings about the bloody collision, just across the Cambodian border, of a gang of rapacious bandits and a fleeing force of Viet Cong, the marauding nuisance and the military enemy made, after a little third-party prodding, to cancel each other out in the place they both consider sanctuary (p. 45); there is the snatch of the VC colonel that becomes possible only when his consort has been supplied with perhaps the only diaphragm in what has been until recently Madam Nhu's Catholic Vietnam and hence is assured she will not accidentally conceive a Viet Cong baby (p. 123); there is the scam that brings about the medical evacuation of fourteen children wounded by trigger-happy South Vietnamese, the joke of going one up on the housecats who write the regulations by listing the casualties quite rightly as "VC POW's" (p. 250).

There is repeatedly, at the conclusion of nearly every episode of *The Green Berets*, the sense of a war that is already turning into a grotesque parody of itself. It is there in the knowing smile and the handshake, the triumph of the mission, the affirmation of comradeship in the right, the vanquishing, albeit through somewhat irregular methods, of the bad guys, whoever they may be, for another day.

The Green Berets does turn out to be "a book of truth," truth about a war fought somewhere between *Catch-22* and the comic books, between Conrad's *Heart of Darkness* and the wondrous nowhere world of the Saturday-afternoon movies. It images again and again the strange, adolescent, death-trip fantasy that was to come. There it was indeed: the camp of strikers, culled from the nether world of Saigon's jails, lodged securely in the old French fort, once held by the Viet Minh, then again by the French, now an outpost of the South Vietnamese Special Forces, the LLDBG, and their American advisors, who know them better as "the lousy little dirty bugouts" (p. 78); "the zoo," a mad, horny gibbon in a cage, performing for the amusement of the camp's irregular troops businesslike anal rapes on chickens (pp. 127–28); the nightly movie, in its way, the master image of it all—

It was a Cinemascope production, but the camp's 16-mm movie projector was not equipped with a Cinemascope lens so the Cowboys, Indians and horses all were long and thin. However, the strikers loved the action and identified themselves with it. When the Indians appeared the strikers screamed "VC," and when the soldiers or cowboys came to the rescue the Nam Luong irregulars vied with each other in shouting out the number of their own strike-force companies. [P. 132]

The Nam Luong Irregulars: a weird amalgam of boot-camp maggots, with their childlike mockery of training-unit esprit, and the simian hordes of Oz; of overwrought kids at a Saturday flick and the bloodthirsty thieves, thugs, consumptives, syphilitics, and Saigon underworld slime they really were. The Nam Luong Irregulars were the war in all the shame and sordor and trumped-up foolishness of it, makeshift second-rate insanity, wrong and misbegotten from the start.

The author of *The Green Berets*, in his disconcerting literalness, his seeming unconcern for the grotesque, melodramatic irony of much that he reports, finally tells the truth about Vietnam through a kind of strange reality overkill, a truth perhaps truer than any he had envisioned. Norman Mailer, on the other hand, in *Why Are We in Vietnam?*, set out to tell that truer truth from the beginning through the assumption of a calculated literariness, the attempt to write a book that was about the war finally by being about anything but the war, the putative subject of the work's title mentioned directly only on the last page. In large measure he succeeds, by means that are as duplicitously roundabout in an aesthetic sense as Moore's are innocently direct. Moreover, he arrives at a similar point. His Vietnam, too, will lie somewhere between *Catch-22* and the latest version of cowboys and gooks, between apocalyptic madness and plain lurid melodrama.

Coming to us at once through the doubled echolalic voices of D. J., scion of a redneck magnate in Dallas, and deejay, a crippled genius in Harlem, and extending its symbolic geography from New York to Texas to the Brooks Range of Alaska, the last of the last frontiers, the book is media event, X-rated soap opera, adventure romance, epic quest, pastoral idyll, ultimate macho power and death trip. It *is* Vietnam, summoned up at its very springs in the American soul.

Dominating the early portions of the narrative is the image of D. J.'s father, Rusty Jellicoe. A kind of ultimate American paterfamilias, looking like "a high-breed crossing between Dwight D. Eisenhower and Henry Cabot Lodge" (p. 31), he is the conquering spirit of native enterprise, the walking conglomerate, taking orders, the narrator tells us, only from the "G.P.A."—"who, in case you forget," he goes on, "is the Great

Plastic Asshole" (p. 37). Proud, competitive, violent, his tycoon bravado barely masking a dark inner reserve of sexual fear and self-doubt, he makes up by extending ever outward the reach of corporate conquest, the surrogate projection of self finally merging with the expansionist aspirations of the nation-state, ultimately peddling plastic reality "out where the reindeer run and the flying fishes try out their flying CIA fucks past Mandalay" (p. 30). He is one of the people who has brought us Vietnam.

Introducing Rusty, his wife Alice Hallie Lee Jellicoe (Deathrow Jellicoe, the narrator calls her [p. 12]), D. J., and his black Harlem counterpart, the novel spends its early stages in a domestic interlude, its focus moving back and forth between a surreal version of one man's family—Hallie on her Jewish psychiatrist's couch, half whore, half inviolate Texas lady, expounding on her husband and his share in "the sexual peculiarities of red-blooded men" (p. 12), her troubled son "Ranald," and Tex Hyde, his unsavory, death-tainted comrade—and the obscene, angry blather of a "Spade" who is a "Shade," a "Shade of the White Man" (p. 26), an American other with a "horror" in him (p. 26), "some genius brain up in Harlem pretending to write a white man's fink fuck book in revenge" (p. 27).

Presently the work shifts, however, to its major scene of action, the Brooks Range of Alaska, America's final wilderness. There is played out a stoned contemporary variation on the Leatherstocking Tales mixed with Frederick Jackson Turner, as Rusty, two corporate sycophants known to us as Medium Asshole Pete and Medium Asshole Bill, D. J., and Tex Hyde, undertaker's son and half-Nazi, half-Indian bred to "old rawhide Texas ass" (p. 17), accompany their guide Big Luke Fellinka and his assistant Ollie the Indian Water Beaver on a hunt that is at once a remembrance of a violent expansionist past and a prophecy of the savage technowar soon to be fought in the jungles of Vietnam. Armed with a storehouse of exquisite weaponry, the hunters lay waste to the life of the wild. They butcher wolves, caribou, and bighorn sheep, killing heedlessly and sloppily, dealing out brutal, large, ugly wounds. Their guides mouthing pieties about life in the wilderness, yet altogether sold out to technology, they chase wounded prey across the landscape in helicopters, landing only to come in for kills that as often as not they finally botch. One grizzly, the ultimate prize they have come to find, Rusty misses altogether; another, spotted soon after, dies of pure firepower, of what Big Luke calls "massive shock" (p. 119). So all of wild nature shudders at what Alfred Kazin, addressing the real war imaged in this symbolic one, can describe only as "the manic plenitude of American destructiveness."[6]

In one last attempt to hold on to something of moral manhood and the original values of earth, Rusty and D. J., father and son, abandon the hunt and try to seek the grizzly unaided and on foot, but it is too late. The American eagle, as in a wilderness soliloquy Rusty delivers to his son, has turned out to be a foul scavenger, an agent of torture delighting in its own cruelty, and he himself proves too "used up" (p. 133) to resist his own enlistment in the service of senseless death. He, too, is a foul blight upon all nature, his son discovers, in a crucial last encounter. There, suddenly, is the bear, like Faulkner's "old Priam, reft of his old wife and outlived his children."[7] They wound it and then follow its blood trail like "combat men flushing out a sniper" (p. 144). D. J. finds it first, sees it dying, sitting Buddha-like in a red saucer of its own blood, a great peace in its eyes, something enigmatic and beautiful and wild, something like "a laugh as if between the millstones of two huge pains" (p. 145). Like the vast primordial unknown, it sits, a message from beyond, as Rusty, unable to hold back the power of inborn American overkill, fires. At this instant, in its eyes D. J. sees "all forgiveness gone" (p. 147). In them he reads the message that he cannot know, after a collective national frenzy of overkill in Asia, the frontier beyond the frontier, will also be Vietnam: "Baby, you haven't begun" (p. 147).

Now it remains for D. J. to master what he alone has seen. With Tex, he ventures forth into the wilderness one last time. "Hunter-fucker-fighters" (p. 157) together as they have always been, they strip down, discard their weapons and equipment, attempt to get to the source, the "crystal receiver of the continent" (p. 172). Seeking purification, they become at one with their wilderness prey. Like the creatures of the wild, and, by implication, the small hunted men in the jungles an ocean away, they flee the helicopters sent to search them out. In certain moments, they do seem truly on the verge of communion with some primordial truth of being—the wolf, the eagle, the grizzly, the great migrating flocks of birds, the "last moose of the North" (p. 197) all tell D. J. "that a secret was near, some mystery in the secret of things" (p. 196)—but it is too late here as well. Purification is beyond them. The message they see is clear: "God was a beast, not a man, and God said 'Go out and kill—fulfill my will, go and kill'" (p. 203).

So it will be henceforth. Repositories of the whole guilt-haunted history of the American soul, its violations, its greeds, its lusts, its worshippings at the altar of technocorporate progress—true children, in sum, of the republic, the modern nation-state—they are "never to be near as lovers again, but killer brothers" (p. 204). It is as prophesied. "We're off to see the wizard in Vietnam," D. J. chortles on the last page. "Vietnam, hot damn" (p. 208).

Earlier in the work, in a rare moment of pontification, the narrator has ventured to define comedy as opposed to tragedy. "Comedy," he says, "is the study of the unsound actions of the cowardly under stress, just as tragedy is equal study time of the brave under heroic but enigmatic, reverberating, resonant conditions of loss" (p. 81). In a word, he defines both his book and the war bodied forth through massive and complex symbolic implication within its pages. *Why Are We in Vietnam?*, the title asks, and the work supplies at least the beginnings of an answer in terms of an American vision where comedy and tragedy have become hopelessly commingled. To put it another way, the dominant vision here (this time by calculated aesthetic intention), as it was in *The Green Berets*, is irony. This is true in both a dramatic sense and also, most importantly, in terms of overall perspective as well, the means by which the drama itself is rendered. The voice of Vietnam that speaks here is D. J., "Grand Synthesizer of the Modern Void" (p. 152), as he styles himself, aware of his task of sense-making, aware also of how it arises from "the frustrated impulse of a general desire to improve the creation" (p. 152). Here, as in so many cases of Vietnam writing to come, out of the inherent irony of the experience itself would come the appropriate means of its articulation. The matter of the thing would find a reality truer than the truth alone in the literary means of its telling.

In light of what has been said thus far, it would seem incorrect then to suggest that even much of early American writing about Vietnam labors too long with problems of cultural or literary preconception (or for that matter, as one writer has recently suggested, with the shadows cast by previous Western interpreters of Indochina such as André Malraux or Graham Greene, with their essentially fixed or "prior" assumptions of insight).[8] Preexisting myths and conventions of form, even in their frequent appropriation and acknowledgment, become at most part of a first step toward new kinds of sense-making suited to the peculiarities of the experience at hand.

Accordingly, a good number of various other early attempts to come to literary terms with the experience of Vietnam involved conscious attempts to test out the limits of possibility, to define an available range of form and mode. As there would be all along, there was of course a good deal of soaring *and* sinking, forays into the experimental sublime and retreats into the steamy seriousness of the quotidian and even the outright banal.

In prose fiction, for instance, there were the expected attempts at radical adventuring, chances taken essentially at writing *Catch-22* about *Catch-22*. There was the strange exoticism of Asa Baber's *The Land of a Million Elephants*, the Kafkaesque bleakness of John Sack's *M*, the surreal nightmare fantasy of William Eastlake's *The Bamboo Bed*. There were the "What if?" books: William Crawford Woods's *The Killing Zone*, mentioned earlier, a training-camp mystery spiked with live ammunition, a technowar fable of things gone deadly wrong; Irwin R. Blacker's *Search and Destroy*, the account of a raid into North Vietnam that prophesied in terms of somewhat eerie specifics—a prime case of life getting hopelessly tangled up with art—one actually conducted several years later; and John Briley's *The Traitors*, the tale of a group of American GIs captured by the enemy and enlisted in a bizarre, futile undercover mission to end the war, a mission in which they are all slaughtered save one who is last seen being absorbed once more into the dark jungle verge. There was also one compelling attempt at philosophical fable in Victor Kolpacoff's *The Prisoners of Quai Dong*, a vision of the prison camp and interrogation room—torturers and tortured and witnesses alike all "prisoners" of the war—as master symbol of what one interpreter has called "the metaphysical darkness of our times" at large.[9]

There were also, of course, in the years before 1970, a good number of attempts to write rather more conventional novels of the war, novels in the tradition of Crane, Hemingway, James Jones, or the younger Norman Mailer. The most significant and accomplished of these—as might be expected, mainly because of a sophisticated consciousness on the part of their authors about new possibilities of relationship between literary artifice and experiential truth-telling—were James Crumley's *One to Count Cadence* and David Halberstam's *One Very Hot Day*. Others, of varying degrees of achievement, included Daniel Ford's *Incident at Muc Wa*, Gene D. Moore's *The Killing at Ngo Tho*, C. T. Morrison's *The Flame in the Icebox*, and Tom Tiede's *Coward*. To these could be added *Count Your Dead*, a closely observed and perceptive depiction of the American experience by John Rowe, an Australian, and *The Lion Heart*, the work of a British journalist and historian named Alan Clark.[10]

Completing the spectrum of narrative, and often resembling the works of fiction described in their frequent recourse, conscious and otherwise, to essentially "novelistic" strategies, were first-person accounts of various kinds, their basic approaches ranging from reportage and analysis to more personal forms of witness-bearing such as the memoir, the journal, and the diary. Works of the first sort included Richard Tregaskis's *Vietnam Diary*, Donald Duncan's *The New Legions*, Ward Just's *To What End*,[11] and Martin Russ's *Happy Hunting*

Ground. Reports of a more closely personal nature included Charles Coe's *Young Man in Vietnam*, Larry Hughes's *You Can See a Lot Standing under a Flare in the Republic of Vietnam*, David Parks's *G.I. Diary*, and Samuel Vance's *The Courageous and the Proud*,—the last two concentrating specifically on the experience of the black soldier in the war. Finally, there was also David Douglas Duncan's combination of narrative and photodocumentary entitled *War without Heroes.*[12]

Whatever their ostensible qualities of perspective and mode, the narrative works, predictably, that got closest to Vietnam from the beginning were those that somehow either started out with or shortly came upon a recognition, given the peculiarities of their special task of sense-making, of the essential interchangeability of art and life—an explicit, centralizing vision of the literary process as self-conscious heuristic, a medium not of predication but rather of complex creative discovery. The point can be readily demonstrated through the comparison of two passages, one from William Eastlake's *The Bamboo Bed*, perhaps the most overtly "artificial" of all the early novels of Vietnam, and the other from Ward Just's *To What End*, unquestionably one of the most concrete, accurate, and fully realized "factual" narratives of the same period.

Eastlake begins his novel with a spare, matter-of-fact account of what seems to be the suicide of an exquisite French-Indochinese courtesan on hearing news of the death of her lover, an American ranger named Clancy. "Madame Dieudonne arose stark and stripped," he writes, "in her underground villa at 0600 as was her wont, turned on the shortwave radio and heard the report from Laos that Captain Clancy was dead, then she walked, still naked, to her jewel box, removed a small, black, heavy object, raised it to her head and blew her pretty

French brains out" (p. 1). Then, abruptly, he interjects a warning, "*Pas vrai*. Not true." He continues: "That's the way the papers had it, but they did not get it right. They never do. The newspapers seldom get anything right because they are not creative. Life is an art" (p. 1). To be sure, the narrator adds in a moment, "The newspapers made a good story. But there is a better one. The truth" (p. 7). Just as "life is an art," art, we are led to infer, is a way of making the world yield up life in some new and unexpected fullness of actuality. Here, in calling attention to the artificiality of literary endeavor, the novel's narrator in the same moment makes his claim upon a vision of the truth somehow truer than anything a pure documentation of the "real" can conceivably provide.

Yet the same lesson, Ward Just notes midway in *To What End*, a work almost obsessive in its painstaking concern for the realistic and particular, could also hold its tantalizing obverse. As one inclined to reach toward what seemed the truer truth of literary sense-making, one immediately felt in the same moment the sharp tug of realities wholly without definition as anything but themselves, themselves only, nothing more, nothing less.

So Just reflected as he looked on what he had thus far observed and reported:

Somewhere in all of that I thought there was a fine novel. Hiep, Hathaway and Hollingsworth, the Cuban and the lieutenant, were all good novel people, and so was the sarcastic sergeant who talked about what a fine thing, a *good* thing, it was to be "a big red *one*." There was a book as good as *A Farewell to Arms* in the stories, if you had the wit to see it and the imagination to generalize from it. But it never worked out that way, and one was left with another fragment, another note toward a definition of the Vietnam war. One hoped that it would be useful, writing about the kid who quit in the middle of a fight, or the casual murder of a Vietnamese cafe owner in Binh Dinh province (by a half-dozen drunk Ruff-Puffs), the American provincial representative in the Delta whose sister lived in the Congo and collected the effects of dead Belgian mercenaries, the poor boy named Truman Shockley who was shot through the heart by a sniper one afternoon just as he lit a Lucky Strike cigarette. I used Shockley in four different ways in four different stories, to make four different points. But it was only a fragment. I didn't have any more to go on than his name, and the memory of the shots and his falling, and the attempts to revive him. [P. 165]

The discovery of sense-making made by both writers is perhaps best summarized in the epigraph chosen by Just from Harold Pinter. At issue is an idea of "verification" that Pinter chooses to define as a central problem in art and life alike, one indeed that cannot even begin to be resolved until the two things are conceived of in terms of their creative mutuality. Verification, he writes, must be a kind of "truth-i-fi-cation" in the fullest sense of the term possible. Our wish for it, he continues, "is understandable." Unfortunately, the wish "cannot always be satisfied. There are no hard distinctions between what is real and what is unreal, nor between what is true and what false. The thing is not necessarily true or false. It can be both true and false."

It is precisely this realization that characterizes the most significant and accomplished early fiction of the war and makes it prophetic of similar work to come. This is so across a whole conceivable range between report and invention. Were one to choose three important early novels of Vietnam, the list would surely include *The Bamboo Bed*, *One to Count Cadence*, and *One Very Hot Day*, works spanning what can be thought of as some likely range of passage between artifice and actuality. Yet not only do they have in common an understanding of the essential interchangeability of the "real" and the "unreal," the "true" and the "false"; they also make it a central premise of literary method. As works of art, they seem to subscribe to a vision supplied, appropriately, by Melville's *The Confidence-Man*, perhaps the locus classicus on the problem at hand. "It is with fiction as with religion," Melville's narrator tells us. "It should present another world, and yet one to which we feel the tie."[13]

Eastlake's novel, for instance, makes its meaning by quite literally flaunting its own artificiality (besides all the talk of art-consciousness, there is the style, terse, sequential, linear, down even to the interpolated gallicism, pure Hemingway, at once a parodic jab and a gesture of homage for the earlier master). Establishing in its first paragraphs the relationship between truth and literary falsehood as a central thematic issue, it suggests that there may be other and even better ways for fictions to accrue factual authority than by claiming it outright. American ranger captains, wearing Roman helmets and bringing their own drummer boys, do not drop from the sky near the villas of their French-Vietnamese, gift-from-God mistresses. Medevac pilots do not spend their time between dust-offs switching the helicopter on automatic pilot and copulating above the battlefield with compliant partners such as Nurse Janine Bliss. Flower children, sixties-version San Francisco, can have no plausible novelistic reason for wandering about in a jungle no-man's-land. Hard-bitten colonels with disabled arms do not fly around the country firing machine guns with their teeth in the company of redneck pilots named Billy Joe. Eastlake forswears verisimilitude from the outset. The truth of Vietnam in *The Bamboo Bed* lies in the book's unerring "literary" suggestiveness.

The truth of Eastlake's vision of the war, to put it another way, is art-truth. It is something that in its fashion just may be truer, he proposes, than facts themselves can ever be. For in this case, he makes clear, it is also much the truth of collective mythic consciousness. Captain Clancy, the American, the hero-out-of-date (something he himself comes to realize as he ultimately lies there dying in the jungle), is indeed "the biggest thing since Custer" (p. 251). He carries, an old friend rightly observes, "the secret of the war" (p. 71). His mission is American history. It is the old national habit, charging up the idiot hill, volunteering to take Paradise (p. 280). But here is not Paradise, but only the beyond. Against the backdrop of silent, impassive Asia, America's eternal adolescent innocence spends itself in terrible self-induced explosion. It is Joseph Conrad, with background music by Jimi Hendrix or the Animals or the Mothers of Invention. At the last, imaging the book that bears its name, the helicopter called the Bamboo Bed makes a final recovery, the bodies of Clancy and a Vietnamese adversary locked in a death embrace. It rises from the jungle, seeks the sun, and takes struggling flight, only to plummet back into the steaming wet dark: "The Vietnamese sun bore down with such magnitude in the abiding Asian forest that the butterfly, the Bamboo Bed, the insect in the vastness, was for long seconds visible until it once again came into the long shadow of the monsoon and was forever lost, disappeared, eaten by tigers, enveloped in the gentle, tomblike Asian night" (p. 350).

Although one can claim a great deal for *The Bamboo Bed*, one must also note that its merits are often a key to its defects as well. As a model of self-conscious artifice, it would be much improved on, for instance, in works such as Gustav Hasford's *The Short-Timers* or Tim O'Brien's *Going after Cacciato*, where elements of surreal fantasy are more authoritatively interfused with a sense of close realistic observation, evidence of having considered Vietnam on its own terms as experience as well. Somewhat too often here, as an example of the new novel of war as written by Heller, Vonnegut, or Pynchon, Eastlake's book seems less concerned with Vietnam than with invoking the paranoid "logic" of its models through various forms of intellectual and aesthetic conceit. It is full of pregnant one-line profundity, non-sequitur nonsense that reads like a textbook in the modern absurd. Example:

> "Why are you shooting at them?"
> "Because they are shooting at us."
> "Who is shooting at whom?"
> "Everyone is shooting at each other."
> "Why?"
> "War." [P. 177]

This is close to a literal transcription of dialogue from the early pages of *Catch-22*. *The Bamboo Bed*, like John Sack's *M*, a work somewhat similar in its merits and excesses (Sack even has an eiron-protagonist named Demirgian) succeeds least when it tries to be *Catch-22* instead of itself. How greatly it does succeed, however, in those moments when it concentrates its power of art-truth on Vietnam *as experience* is underscored by its ironic similarity to Sack's book, which in its initial form of publication in *Esquire* was called a documentary.

There was the real "catch," the one more pertinent to the experience at hand, the likeness of two books so ostensibly far apart in mode and intention. In significant portions of his narrative, for instance, Sack places much of the burden of meaning on his own collection of one-liners, and often the sense of hopeless absurdity embodied in their grim matter-of-factness outstrips anything comparable Eastlake might have offered by way of surreal contrivance:

> "Oh my God!"
>
> "The bullet went through his helmet."
>
> "What have you did?"
>
> "If they're not a VC now, they'll be one later."
>
> "Sir, there's a little girl."
>
> "I finally killed me a gook." [14]

If there is a truth in this experience, both works seem to say, it is often contained in what seems mainly a collection of baffling non sequiturs, sense-defeating fragments. The secret of unriddling a truth even this tentative and partial, moreover, would seem to lie in the attempt to seek out its meanings not simply in life or in art but rather in some creative conflation of both. Here was a way, then, of assembling these fragments, these necessary provisional meanings so as at least to point to a central method and direction whereby other and more complete ones might ultimately be found.

Less radical than *The Bamboo Bed* in its insistence on its own artifice, yet conspicuously dividing its focus between realistic depiction of the war and the attempt on frequent occasions to create a distinct atmosphere of dream, of imaginative invention, of even surreal fantasy, *One to Count Cadence* responds precisely to the foregoing imperative. It locates the truth of Vietnam at once in life—a vision of the experience itself that would become increasingly familiar in its concrete typicality—and in art—a vision of sense-making possibility in this case connecting private consciousness with the larger shapes of collective American myth. The book's narrator, Slag Krummel, as he constantly reminds us, is both himself and a kind of representative aesthetic image of his culture as a whole. He is indeed the walking embodiment of prophetic myth, at once the function of memory and imagining, come to new and complex realization in present actuality. "The past, history, memory," he says, "had always waited for me like a specter. My memory never knew the chains of time." At Pittsburg's landing, at Elkhorn Tavern, on the Upper Brazos, he continues, "I saw and will forever see, the ghosts of men dying, and as I saw I understood, despite the protests of the fallen themselves, that it was heroic, was perhaps the last noble thing" (p. 173). The present, he admits, has changed a good deal of what made it possible to think that, if in fact it should have ever been possible to do so. In a single moment things have been clarified and complicated. If the purpose of this newest call to heroism in Asia seems precisely in its elegiac beauty somewhat more clearly defined, it also—again precisely because the elegy in question is for a myth of culture that has itself from the start been a masterwork of blood-spattered fatal self-deceit—suddenly seems a lot less worth dying for. To be an American now is to know, Krummel writes, that "we are," simply, "the last, the best and the last of the barbarians, the conquerors, the long knives, the jolly green giants of history who move at first across the land with fire and sword, then with transistor radios and toothpaste, seeking not even greener grass, nor even movement itself, but merely senseless turds in the large bowel of history" (p. 227).

In keeping with this growth of awareness, Krummel's war finally turns out to be not so much with the enemy as it is with himself and the warrior mythos that has spawned him. He works at a freewheeling insouciance, a perverse intractability, an attempt to be hard about the ironic, ambivalent hand history has dealt him. His motto, contained in the book's title, is an old army prayer:

> Fuck 'em all but nine—
> Six for pallbearers,
> Two for roadguards,
> And one to count cadence.

Challenged by his mentor, the physician Gallard, to come to terms with his role in one more American war, he responds, "I was raised for a warrior. What would you have me do?" (p. 25). Yet increasingly, for all his self-dramatization, his myth-hungry posturing, he truly is as his friend Joe Morning has said. Like them all, he is the offspring of "millions of comic books and B-movies," the projection of some "Puritan middle-class mind" that always gets "killing mixed up with screwing" (p. 170). He is just another "reactionary moralist" who believes in ghosts (p. 308). Or, as Gallard has put it to him, "Victim of an undeclared war, huh? Fighter for right and humanity?" Maybe better just "killer of small hungry men" (p. 25).

The drift of "history" for Krummel, in both a personal and a representative symbolic sense, comes to a violent and appropriately botched ironic climax on a hillside in Vietnam, after a desperate firefight, when, true to the last to his inborn sense of fated mythic drama, he keeps silent vigil with the corpse of a slain enemy. He has sat through the darkness with his arm around the dead man's shoulders, and now he gets up to continue his warrior mission. As he does, he is mistakenly shot by Dottlinger, the dumb, officious, up-from-the-ranks lieutenant, half overgrown adolescent bully, half banal pathetic clown, who has served throughout the work as a bumbling exemplar

of the mission reduced to terms of the modern word democratic. Here, for all his theorizing on the warrior sublime,
Krummel finds his genuine opposite number. He is undone by
the new apostle of mission in a war where no one finally will
be in charge, where the dominant principle will be the aimless
spirit of the killing itself.

Krummel describes his part in the fated encounter as being
trapped in the end by his fear of the dead rising; and he has as
usual spoken more truth than he knows. By almost getting to
be one of our dead by getting mixed up with one of theirs, he
has come close to acting out what will ultimately be for many
Americans the only story the war will reveal. But he himself
has only begun to pay the price. It is not nearly over yet. As the
book ends, he is back from Laos and the CIA, three years later,
again recovering from wounds. He has been "with the killing"
so long, he says, that he makes people "nervous." He is his
America, and now he has become the war as well. Even if he
survives, there will be no coming back. In a sense, Krummel
can now say of himself what he has said of Joe Morning, run off
to join the Philippine Huks in an attempt to escape the im-
plications of collective mythic consciousness, an attempt as
haunted and perverse as Krummel's to see those same implica-
tions through to the end. "Even if he isn't dead," he concludes,
"he is surely lost" (p. 337).

"Art, History, Life: traitorous knaves," Krummel has written
earlier. "Don't blame me; I'm just their foolish pawn chained
to my machine" (p. 300). Nonetheless, through a calculated artifice, the explicit attempt to place these things in some provisional context of mutually illuminating relationship, he does
finally bring them into a creative balance that yields up new
meanings appropriate to the experience at hand.

Yet so, on the far realistic other end of the literary spectrum, in works such as David Halberstam's *One Very Hot Day*, similar forms of symbiotic relationship could be effected as well. There indeed, it is precisely the linear, impassive, matter-of-fact rendering of the quotidian that somehow cumulatively takes us beyond the real to a vision of waste, futility, and suffering so stark and ritualized as to seem almost iconographic.

What is finally most appalling about the war we see in *One Very Hot Day*, what endows it with its almost archetypal quality of nightmare, is Halberstam's ability to depict the intensity of its utter, soul-killing ordinariness. For Beaupre, the tired, fat, superannuated American captain, and Thuong, the equally weary Vietnamese lieutenant, both of whom stand near some common, numb center of focal consciousness, Vietnam is simply an exhausting, dangerous, despair-ridden continuum. There is heat, fatigue, thirst, anger, fear, frustration, boredom; another brackish, smelly stream to cross; one more attempt to keep feckless, ill-disciplined provisional troops from making noise or bunching up. Punctuation comes only as a booby trap, an ambush, one more piece of death around the corner, and after that, probably just another. It all at a certain point seems so oppressively, insanely circumstantial, so anchored in the quotidian that it strangely begins to take one all the way over to the other side.

Beaupre's response on this day to the dead, for instance, killed in the inevitable ambush, becomes a dismal, free-floating meditation, at once clinical and curiously surreal:

There was a trail of dead Vietnamese. They were scattered in all directions, as if someone with a giant hand had rolled them out like dice. He realized that he did not recognize them or know their names. One of them had been sucking on a sugar cane stalk and the cane was still in his mouth. Beside him was another man with part of his face shot away, he had been caught in the chin and neck. The first burst, Beaupre thought, had obviously been a little high or it might have been worse. Another lay toppled over on his side, with his palm outstretched as if he had been praying; another lay sprawled down, his eyes closed, completely silent, but his transistor radio on, either he had switched it on when he was dying, or else he had violated the noise blackout, the radio was playing their damn singsong music. [P. 195]

His war "over for the day" (p. 215), Beaupre ponders how to write to the wife of his zealous West Point subordinate, Lieutenant Anderson, also killed in the afternoon's action. What to say? That Anderson "had died during a hot walk in the sun, no not that, he had been killed in a battle, yes." Where? Beaupre remembers a name, Ap Than Thoi, that he and his American cohorts use for nowhere places. It is a name from a map, a village that was supposed to be there but wasn't. It is "the missing village" (p. 141). He wants to write that Anderson died "just past Ap Than Thoi" but remembers that the lieutenant, good earnest and literal American, has once explained the joke in a letter to his wife. The name is no good, and neither is the joke: "she knew where Ap Than Thoi was" (p. 216).

Anderson has died someplace just past nowhere on one very hot day. Like the title of the book, it is what one might call a lowercase joke, more dreary and banal and ultimately soul-chilling than any Kafkaesque fantasy one might care to contrive.

This would seem to be precisely the discovery made by Ward Just in the writing of *To What End,* a book presented, unlike Halberstam's, not as fiction but as reportage. The character of perception is nonetheless identical. As Just suggests, it is all there, quite like that, on any given day. It is what happens. No one has to make it up.

The joke is comprehensive. It includes anyone who gets caught up in the war. Volunteering himself in some fit of perverse bravado on a Tiger Force mission with recondos from the 101st Airborne, a mission that rapidly becomes a slaughter for the elite American troops, Just keeps coming face to face with a black GI who collapses in laughter each time he sees him; apace, he considers "the similarity of the soldier and the war correspondent, the basic text for which is Joseph Heller's *Catch-22*." He explains: "On the one hand, no one wants to get ambushed or to be where bullets are fired in anger. On the other, if nothing happens there is no story. If the patrol does not meet the enemy, there is nothing to write about. It becomes a pointless exercise, a long walk under a hot sun. If the patrol does meet the enemy you are likely to be killed or wounded, or at the very least scared to death. *Catch-23*" (p. 181).

Presently, the grim thesis works out. Beginning in simple, spare transcription, it concludes in frozen, awful fulfillment of its own prophetic design:

> "Sheet, I wrote her back she do anything she want."
> "Well, we over here and they're there."
> "Fuck that noise."
> "Yeah."
> "You hear Tomkins get killed?"
> "Yeah?"
> "Sheet, a mine blew him up and there was nuthin' left but nuthin'."
> "Sheet."
> "I tell you, Man, this is some kind of war."

"Crise, I was in a platoon and there's nuthin' left of that platoon now. I'm the only one left."

"Gimme some fruit."

"Trayja fruit for some butts."

"Whyn't you pick up the butts back there when we got 'em?"

"Cause I was on point savin' your ass in case old Charlie come along."

"Gimme the fuckin fruit."

"Three butts."

"Sheet, man, I ain't got but half a pack."

"Goddamn I got to get this weapon *fixed*."

"Hey, Mr. Reporter, what the fuck you doing here?" [P. 182]

The grenades start coming in. Soon, three more Americans are dead and six are wounded. The war goes on. Joseph Heller could have written it, but he could not have written it better, because it was already true.

The unifying feature, then, for all their seeming diversity, of the major Vietnam narratives discussed thus far—the thing that makes them both significant in their own right and prophetic of many important works to come—is the degree to which they all in various ways identify and exploit what could already be seen as a central mode of sense-making. Addressing Vietnam as experience, as opposed to some problem defined in terms of moral, philosophical, or aesthetic abstraction, they nonetheless search out appropriate possibilities for combining life and art, art and life, in new forms of creative symbiosis. They explore the aesthetic possibilities of the quotidian; and in the same moment, they also propose, so to speak, new "quotidian" possibilities of aesthetic as well. For all their openness to traditional literary values, they also suggest, for instance, in a new age of modern mass communication, that a "reality" of Vietnam as TV nightly news with live ammunition could as easily shape itself in the image of other detritus from the great media wasteland—melodrama, sitcom, cartoon, comic book— that the shapes of art that could be expected to reproduce themselves in the life of a generation reared on such second-rate business might not elicit the vision of *Catch-22*, but rather something more like Catch-21½ or ¾ or maybe ⅞.

The attempt to address relationships between life and art, between experiential memory and imaginative invention, through some evolving concept of mediative discovery, a view of the sense-making or fictive process as more than anything else a complex, open-ended heuristic, is not in itself a new idea. The impulse to devise a system of meanings subject to change, to use Frank Kermode's terms, "as the needs of sense-making change,"[15] is perhaps the one common feature of all literary endeavor in an essentially secular age, an age no longer capable of the kinds of unitary belief essential to myth and hence forced to seek meanings provisionally in its best and most characteristic fictions. Neither would the attempt to address this idea of literary process in varying degrees of self-consciousness seem to be much more than a variation, albeit under somewhat peculiar and exacerbated circumstances, on what we have in general come to call the literary spirit of the modern. It is the animating spirit of *Tristram Shandy*, of *Moby-Dick*, of *Remembrance of Things Past*, of *Ulysses*, and in recent decades it has become so dominant as at times to commit critical fashion to the idea of a kind of ultimate metaliterature, a literature devoted wholly to the contemplation of its own processes.

What would seem to be a literary development of considerable analogical value in defining the newness or uniqueness of our writing about Vietnam, especially in its emergent centralizing mode, is the evolution of a concept, appropriately American in its origins, appropriately practical and fact-oriented yet once again making good the prophecy of Toc-queville[16] in its concomitant hospitality to a strange play of high abstraction, that might be best called the idea of a "new realism."[17] It is a mode of experiment that makes something like Norman Mailer's *The Executioner's Song*[18]—essentially a document, the surreal psychobiography of a sad, hungry, irredeemably violent American loser, yet in its complex vision of the problem of sense-making itself, a book very much about the processes of art as well—much of a literary piece with a work of fiction like William Styron's *Sophie's Choice*[19]—from its first word, an art-novel of the highest order, a book about books and their making, yet also a work possessed of the immense human authority that can only come through confronting a sense of the fundamental factualness of experience (in this case, the memory of the Holocaust) in all its terrible weight and plenitude.

It is "creative" mediation so defined, as I will suggest later and in more detail, that endows Michael Herr's *Dispatches*, for all its feel of running over burnt-out fact circuits, brain cells dead of stoned information overload, with what is nonetheless a distinctly new and original architecture of consciousness appropriate to new demands of sense-making; and it is the lack of such an open spirit of mediation that makes so ostensibly similar a work, Gloria Emerson's *Winners and Losers*,[20] always seem to be getting used up on both ends at once—its matter mainly lying there as loaded case history or being oxidized—to use the precise chemical term, sublimated—in the incandescence of the author's abstract moral and philosophical indignation.

This sense of bifurcation, at times, as in Emerson's book, the result of mainly polemical intention, also genuinely cripples some of the less successful early fictions of the war, such as Tom Tiede's *Coward* and C. T. Morrison's *The Flame in the Icebox*. In other cases, the split occurs on more general terms of craft, as in works such as Daniel Ford's *Incident at Muc Wa*, Gene D. Moore's *The Killing at Ngo Tho*, John Briley's *The Traitors*, and Irwin R. Blacker's *Search and Destroy*—all of them intensely "plotted" books in the conventional sense of that term, and hence straining, presumably through some abstract sense of the "strangeness" of the subject at hand, to seem in the same moment conspicuously and even wildly circumstantial.

A kind of broken circuit—a split between moral, philosophical, or aesthetic abstraction on one hand and undifferentiated visions of the concrete and actual on the other—is also an appropriate figure for describing most of early Vietnam drama and poetry. In neither mode could writers seem yet to find a center defined in terms of the creative dialectic already at work in various forms of narrative.

The situation for drama would change presently, in the early 1970s, when a young veteran named David Rabe, responding to his own experience of the Vietnam years, would emerge as one of the most important playwrights of his generation. Prior to the publication of his work, however, most of the Vietnam drama there was remained so thoroughly divided between a kind of arty abstraction and a visceral anger spilling over from the experience of a protest generation in the streets as to make one wonder if that particular split was ever going to be resolved, let alone a play eventually be written about the experience of the war itself.

The only early play, indeed, that came close to achieving the latter end, Arthur Kopit's *Indians*,[21] did so by such lavish indirection that most viewers missed the point. Nonetheless, the point was there, and *Indians*, in its complex symbolic exploration of the war's relationship with a larger body of collective mythic assumption, remains both as literary artifact and inquiry into the process of cultural myth-making itself one of the most singular and accomplished productions of the whole Vietnam era.

The play is very much "about" the war in something of a reversal of the strategy worked to such considerable novelistic success by William Eastlake in *The Bamboo Bed*. Focused on Buffalo Bill's America—and that of General Custer as well, whom the hero invokes as telling him once never to be scared of "makin' a personal comeback" (p. 3)—the play addresses the last American "Indian" wars in terms of their prophetic connection with the latest; and it does so also by summoning up a whole cultural legacy of heroism defined in the ability to deal death. To some degree, Kopit's Cody resembles E. E. Cummings's familiar image: he is a blue-eyed killer, a murderer showman. He is equally in the vein, however, of Cooper's Leatherstocking, to use D. H. Lawrence's apt characterization, as "a saint with a gun."[22] He is a violent, bullheaded, self-torturing do-gooder who actually seems to believe—as will at least one celebrated successor in Vietnam, a young officer standing outside a "friendly" village he has just had leveled by an airstrike—that one can destroy things in order to "save" them.

There was the general connection between *Indians* and the experience of Vietnam. There were also specific ones, however, that at least in retrospect seem more than clear. In one early scene, for instance, a grand duke of Russia, touring the plains, insists that like his hero and guide Buffalo Bill, he must kill a

Comanche. There are no Comanches around. The party is in Missouri, not Texas. Undaunted, he mortally wounds a Sioux. The dying Indian mentions the mistake, but when asked for a translation, Cody instead replies lamely, "He said . . . 'I . . . should have . . . stayed at home in . . . Texas with the rest of my . . . Comanche Tribe'" (p 21). There it was indeed. Later on, in Vietnam, it would be called the TOG rule. TOG: They're Only Gooks.

So it continues throughout the play, even as Cody serves first as hired gun and later as emissary and eventual pawn in a "peace" mission doomed from the start. One keeps hoping that the jokes will stay merely jokes, even as the past continues to turn itself out as present and future. One listens to the dialogue of historical drama and instead seems to hear the captain at Song Be whom Michael Herr recalls lining up his hundred-man patrol and telling him, "Come on, we'll take you out to play Cowboys and Indians" (p. 60). Kopit's "Indian" war persistently images the Vietnam that was and would be.

It does so, moreover, by talking about a war not only as it is actually fought but also as it is conceived of by the shapers of national policy at home. There occur scenes in the work, for instance, in which Ned Buntline, the enterprising reporter, contrives for Cody and Wild Bill Hickok, along with a polyglot spaghetti-western cast, to appear at the White House in a historical play of Buntline's authorship. It is history as bombastic self-parody, punctuated by endless, profane, nonsensical squabbling among the principals. Interrupted in the middle of a grandiose speech by Hickok walking over and staring incredulously in his face, Cody exclaims, "Just *what are* you doin'?" Hickok replies, "What're you doin'?" The impromptu scene continues:

BUFFALO BILL: I'm doin' what I'm doin', that's what I'm doin'!

HICKOK *(To Buntline)*: Always was intelligent.

BUFFALO BILL: I am doin' what my country *wants!* WHAT MY BELOVED COUNTRY *WANTS!*

HICKOK *(To the First Family)*: This . . . is . . . what you want?

FIRST LADY: Absolutely!

OL' TIME PRESIDENT: Best play I've seen in years! [Pp. 36–37]

The play-within-the-play is also one in which an actor playing "Uncas," improvising on the script in a heavy German accent, suggests his own idea of what an Indian is good for: "Being murdered," he says, "is his purpose in life" (p. 38). Yet Buffalo Bill, eventually moving on to leadership of Roughriders of the World, knows the terrible murder-joke of historical play-acting has come brutally real. Like Eastlake's Clancy, he has finally gotten scared of himself. His mixing of the hero business with quasi-patriotic horseplay has somehow gotten out of control. It breeds ghosts. "I dunno' what's happenin' anymore," he says. "Things have gotten . . . *beyond* me. I see them *everywhere*. In the grass. The rocks. The branches of dead trees. . . . Took a drink from the river yesterday an' they were even there, beneath the water, their hands reachin' up, I dunno' whether beggin', or t' . . . drag me under" (p. 68).

In desperation, Cody turns at the last to Hickok, whom he now sees as an exemplar of sanity in a world gone grotesquely, even theatrically wrong, but it is too late. Hickok is now a believer. He is making plans for Buffalo Bill international, a legion of Codys. Consider, he tells his old friend, "the *great national good* . . . that could come from this: some of you, let's say, would concentrate strictly on theatrics. MEANWHILE! *Others* of you would concentrate on purely humanitarian affairs. Save . . . well, not Sitting Bull, but . . . some Indian down in Florida. Another up in Michigan. Perhaps expand into Canada. Mexico. Central America. SOUTH AMERICA! My God, there must be literally *millions* of people who could benefit by your presence! Your . . . *simultaneous presence!*" (p. 70).

In the final two words of the speech lies the unsettling secret of *Indians*. The last joke is not just on Buffalo Bill but on Buffalo Bill's America, a joke of "simultaneous presence" indeed: one endless "Indian" war, waged by myth-haunted heroes out of date, waged in all the wrong ways for all the wrong reasons in a grand tragedy of mass cultural misperception. It is the tragic joke, most recently recapitulated in Vietnam, of our whole collective experience as a people.

Vietnam as subject or problem might be said to be more explicitly "there" than in *Indians* in other early plays such as Ron Cowen's *Summertree* or John Guare's *Muzeeka*,[23] but in neither case would the author achieve the kind of high truth of art reached through Kopit's complex mythic symbology. *Summertree* is about a young man victimized unto death essentially by his decent middle-class values. Taking a chance on a music career, as opposed to a more practical education advocated by his parents, he loses his draft deferment and is inducted into the army and eventually killed in Vietnam. The issues of conscience and cultural value that the play raises, however, often get lost in a mixture of loose staginess and sentimental abstraction. *Muzeeka*, clearly the work of an accomplished experimentalist, involves a self-made tycoon, a purveyor of canned music for dentists' offices and discount stores, who, to escape the banality of domestic routine, joins the army and is sent to Vietnam. There he eventually commits suicide. It is clear that he is meant as a type and example of a whole nation's lapse into historical purposelessness, perhaps of all nations' lapses into such purposelessness in their comings and goings. His last words as he stabs himself are a reprise of his early description of ancient Etruria, the vigorous, innocent forerunner of the first Rome, perhaps in that innocence the only nation ever founded on pure outright joy. But now his words are a more generalized historical death-chant encompassing his own predicament as well. They are the final elegy: "The Etruscans lived and danced about a million years ago and then vanished without a trace like a high curved wave that breaks on the sand and retreats back into the sea. Poof. Vanish. Splash" (p. 81).

Muzeeka, far more than *Summertree*, has many such moments when there arise large and important perceptions of Vietnam and of its prospective meanings for our culture as a whole. For all its symbolic range and ambition, however (Argue, the protagonist, is an acronym of the playwright himself), it also lapses frequently into a somewhat random mixture of abstruse "living theater" experimentalism and didactic harangue. This would also seem to have been the case, as the critic Robert Asahina has noted, with other early works such as Megan Terry's *Viet Rock* which were performed but did not see print. In seeking to combine avant-garde aestheticism with experiential relevance, they often succeeded on one count only by way of defeating their purpose with regard to the other.[24]

The breakdown that characterizes much of Vietnam drama, particularly in the early stages, between Vietnam considered mainly as formalistic conceit and Vietnam as pure happening, undifferentiated experiential event, is a good model for much of the early poetry of the war as well. The great majority of it was the product of the antiwar movement and thus not only the work of people at some remove, for all their moral passion (the antiwar soldier-poets would come along presently), from the experience itself but also of people for the most part associated with the academy or the liberal intelligentsia. The names often associated with early Vietnam poetry were familiar: Bly, Levertov, Lowell, Duncan, Ginsberg, Lowenfels. But it was never really their war. It was their cause. Their Vietnam, as their poetry shows, was mainly the product of moral, philosophical, ideological argument. It could not have been otherwise. Polemic, insofar as it supplies a vision of ideas articulated in such radical relief as to inspire wholesale commitment, can only be a form of high abstraction. Its concern with concrete actuality will only be to the degree that it illustrates the validity of that commitment. It is no surprise then, as a recent critic, Robert Shaw, has observed, that much of the early poetry of Vietnam remained caught between "diatribe and "documentary," static, predictable, almost ritualized in its own dividedness.[25]

Even a poem so strong, compelling, and original in its own creative energies, for instance, as Robert Bly's "The Teeth Mother Naked at Last"[26] still seems a good part of the time a cross between hectoring lesson and angry newsreel. It is one thing to say:

This is what it's like for a rich country to make war
this is what it's like to bomb huts (afterward described as "structures")
this is what it's like to kill marginal farmers (afterwards described as
    "Communists")

this is what it's like to watch the altimeter needle going mad

Baron 25, this is 81. Are there any friendlies in the
area? 81 from 25, negative on the friendlies. I'd like you to
take out as many structures as possible located in those
trees within 200 meters east and west of my smoke mark.

If anything holds the poem together at this point, it is the un-conscious terrible music of the transcribed conversation be-tween pilots. It is quite another thing, however, to write later on:

> If a child came burning, you would dance on a lawn,
> trying to leap into the air, digging into your cheeks,
> you would ram your head against the wall of your bedroom
> like a bull penned too long in his moody pen—
>
> If one of those children came toward me with both hands
> in the air, fire rising along both elbows,
> I would suddenly go back to my animal brain,
> I would drop on all fours screaming,
> my vocal chords would turn blue, so would yours,
> It would be two days before I could play with my own children again.

For all their flirtation with the stock imagery of protest, the lat-ter stanzas are remarkable both in their originality of imagina-tive statement and in their intense physical immediacy. The important words in them are "you," "your," "yours," words that force themselves outward beyond the boundaries of either po-lemical argument or documentary exposé. One truly did not have to go to Vietnam to bring the experience home in litera-ture. Addressed to the experience *as experience* in the fullness of its terrible human commonality, the work could be done anywhere, as it surely was here.

This is also true of much of the best writing included in Wal-ter Lowenfels's *Where Is Vietnam?*,[27] in many ways a represen-tative selection of early poems against the war. Again, those poems that succeed most do so by addressing Vietnam as com-mon experience and making its meanings insofar as possible the property of the national consciousness at large. So, for instance, with the fusion of this sort worked by Galway Kinnell's "Vapor Trail Reflected in the Frog Pond." No angry preachments here, or rote images of gentle, bewildered "marginal farmers" cowering in paddies as Phantoms streak overhead on a gun run. Rather this, immediate, inevitable, here before anyone has to be told it has come home:

The old look on: their
thick eyes
puff and foreclose by the moon. The young, heads
trailed by the beginnings of necks
shiver,
in the guarantee they shall be bodies.

In the reflection
of the sky in the frog pond the vapor trail
of a SAC bomber creeps.

I hear its drone, drifting, high up
in immaculate ozone.

Meticulous, concrete, precisely crafted, it is all there: the ancient pond; the wizened elders; the young, new bodies in the cold wet; from the water skyward, the contrail, the jet, bringer of the arclight, high in the clean ether. And somewhere, rising above this all, the America-song, a patriotic travesty, a hymn of praise gone deadly and terrible:

And I hear America singing, her varied carols I hear:
Crack of deputies' rifles practicing their aim on stray dogs at night
sput of cattleprod,
TV groaning at the smells of the human body,

curses on the soldier as he poisons, burns, grinds, and stabs
the eternal rice of the world,
with open mouth, crying strong, hysterical curses.

It is in a sense Kinnell's version of *Why Are We in Vietnam?*, pure media overload, all coming across at once in tortured cacophony, the new song of Walt Whitman's republic. It is the answer. Meanwhile:

And by rice paddies in Asia
bones
wearing a few shadows
walk down a dirt road, smashed
bloodsuckers on their heel,
shoulder blades unpitted by old feather-holes
hand rivered
by the blue, erratic wanderings of the blood
knowing the flesh a man throws down in the sunshine
dogs shall eat
and the flesh that is upthrown shall be seized by birds.

Here is the poet's final truth of the war, a kind of pure distillation, an image of an image. Beyond even the loud-mouthed horror, there is something more horrific, the spectral procession of the legions of death toward the final silence of extinction.

Were one to look for the early soldier-poets of Vietnam, in the beginning it was most likely one would encounter instead the work of those members of the war generation who had somehow found it possible to remain at home and make the fight *against* the war the focus of their art. Something more akin to the trench poetry of the Great War or the work of young

American poets of World War II such as Dickey, Shapiro, and Jarrell was still being written, however, although a first book-length collection—*Winning Hearts and Minds: Poems by Vietnam Veterans*—would not see publication until 1972. Published in the same year, although likewise written during the earlier period of large-scale American involvement, was the first major volume by an individual poet, *Obscenities*, by Michael Casey.[28]

What often characterizes both texts (Casey is also included in the veterans' anthology), along with similar poetry appearing before 1970 in isolated collections and journals, is a somewhat predictable division between what might be best described as a dogged concreteness, an attempt to render the experience of the war in all its brute sensory plenitude, and what could be called notes toward a new mythic iconography, attempts to devise new images for a new experience, so to speak, images fierce and unsettling in their bitter originality of imaginative invention.

Typical of the concrete mode is W. D. Ehrhart's "Vietnam—February 1967":

> Air heavy with rain and humidity,
> Sky full of ominous clouds,
> Dank smell of refuse,
> Mosquitoes and flies like carpets on the wind.
>
> Patchwork quilt of rice paddies,
> Winding rivers and swollen streams,
> Water buffalo lumbering through the fields,
> High mountains on the horizon.
>
> Thundering roar of aircraft on the prowl,
> Roads clogged with troops and trucks,

> Distant growl of artillery.
> Crackling whine of small arms.
>
> Ramshackle busses crowded with people
> Bamboo huts with straw-thatched roofs,
> Women bearing baskets from the market;
> A ragged child stares at passing soldiers.

It is a prose poem, really, even a prosaic poem, relentlessly methodical and unambitious in its enumeration of particulars. Its character of diction and image, except, perhaps, for one mildly interesting figure—"mosquitoes and flies like carpets on the wind"—is unoriginal and even trite. It seems to run on mainly in the dogged hope that the concrete will yield up some hoarded vision of unifying truth.

An example of the second mode, a kind of symbolic adventuring in search of similar epiphany, is Basil T. Paquet's "Night Dust-off":

> A sound like hundreds of barbers
> stropping furiously, increases;
> suddenly the night lights,
> flashing blades thin bodies
> into red strips
> hunched against the wind
> of a settling slickship.
>
> Litters clatter open,
> hands reach in
> into the dark belly of the ship
> touch toward moans,
> they are thrust into a privy,
> feeling into wounds,

> the dark belly all wound,
> all wet screams riven limbs
> moving in the beaten night.

As the voice and the vision of the first poem were almost ploddingly quotidian, this one in contrast is composed in an elaborate kind of art-speech, a distracting hodgepodge of fractured syntax and strange figurative ellipsis. It is as enigmatic in its artifice as the other in its ordinariness.

Some early poems did occasionally achieve a kind of mediation between these two extremes. One is Larry Rottmann's "The Weather of Vietnam":

> There are two kinds of weather in Vietnam
> Hot and dry and
> Hot and wet
>
> During the hot and dry
> The dust is as fine as talcum powder
> And hangs like a gritty mist in the air
>
> During the hot and wet
> The monsoon blows so hard
> That it rains sideways.

The tone of the poem, if somewhat wry, is still matter-of-fact, and the character of its craft seemingly unambitious. The image of a "gritty mist," for instance, just saves the second stanza from being merely trite. The central figure of the third stanza, however, rain falling sideways, does seem genuinely original and arresting, but it does not violate the work's essential concreteness of vision. Indeed, it grows rather naturally out of that concreteness of vision in the way that some similar, more famous images in American literature—Huck Finn's description of his father's face, for instance, as "tree toad white"[29] or Stephen Crane's "red sun . . . pasted in the sky like a wafer"[30]—do in fact change our way of looking at things forever while nonetheless reassuring us of their grip on a sense of the common, the specific, the indisputably actual.

This organic sense of mediating perspective—quite similar to that I have described previously in connection with the best of early Vietnam narrative—is what makes Michael Casey's work the first really significant step forward toward a major poetry of the war as experience, a poetry also to be elaborated further in books such as John Balaban's *After Our War* and Bruce Weigl's *A Romance*.[31] A poem of Casey's similar, for instance, to the one I have just discussed in the way it establishes a kind of natural reciprocality between the quotidian and the aesthetic and vice versa is "A Bummer":

> We were going single file
> Through his rice paddies
> And the farmer
> Started hitting the lead track
> With a rake
> He wouldn't stop
> The TC went to talk to him
> And the farmer
> Tried to hit him too
> So the tracks went sideways
> Side by side
> Through the guy's fields
> Instead of single file
> Hard On, Proud Mary

Bummer, Wallace, Rosemary's Baby
The Rutgers Road Runner
and
Go Get Em—Done Got Em
Went side by side
Through the fields
    If you have a farm in Vietnam
And a house in hell
Sell the farm
And go home.

Here is a poem about the experience of Vietnam that genuinely does make its own creative design, opens out and
completes itself along the course of its own inevitability. An
incident of war, at once pathetically real and almost ludicrous
in its arresting absurdity: a peasant beating with a rake on an
armored personnel carrier running point on a trail of destruction through his fields. Suddenly, and for no particular reason,
there comes the pitiless brute response. It is a charge on line
against an enemy rice paddy, a senseless procession of wanton,
arrogant waste, a punishment for the crime of trying to endure.
The America that has brought it to pass stands imaged in the
rude poetry of the names the GIs have painted on their ma-
chines: there is the predictable bit of adolescent sexual swag-
ger; a popular song, half country, half grinding rock; a word for
a bad trip; a right-wing, deep-South demagogue; a movie about
demonic possession; a New Jersey avatar of the most popular
cartoon character on Saturday-morning TV; a sporty way of
sounding like God's own gift to death, the badass killer on the
road. A quick apothegm makes the figure complete, distills its
meanings into a new maxim for a whole misbegotten war.

A similar inevitability of poetic statement, the arrival at a truth of art that is in the same moment altogether a truth of common experience, characterizes "Hoa Binh" ("Peace"):

> August thirty-first
> Stanley was all excited
> She just made eighteen
> And got to vote
> For the first time
> There were sixteen slates
> To vote for
> In Vietnam that year
> And every slate's poster
> Said that
> That slate
> Wanted Hoa Binh
> From voting
> She came back to me
> All excited
> Casee
> I vote for Hoa Binh
> That's nice, Stanley
> I did too
> Back in Hoa Ky
> I hope your vote counts

Here, as in "A Bummer," the terms in which Casey establishes the poem's basic situation in themselves offer an arresting combination of the concrete and matter-of-fact with the strange and even slightly ludicrous, a combination that seems here and often throughout the literature of Vietnam somehow most appropriate to the experience. There is the girl Stanley, the name itself a GI joke, no doubt—in this case, as we learn from another poem, a young MP matron, but someone who could as easily be a housegirl, or a laundress, or a civilian KP or a PX cashier, or a waitress at the EM club, or maybe just another whore. She trills her sad innocent hope that something she has done can help the war to end: "Casee / I vote Hoa Binh." In counterpoint, there comes the larger, more final wisdom that perhaps Vietnam and America are not so different after all. In both places, the country where the war is fought and the country that seems bent on making sure it continues to be fought, Hoa Binh—Peace—would seem to be only an election lie, a word on a ballot, a common geopolitical fiction in a world where Stanleys and Casees alike remain equally helpless ciphers in a general disaster.

Repeatedly in Casey's best poems, the concrete and the quotidian are made to yield up what seem to strike even the poet himself at times as startling and profoundly original truths of art. "To Sergeant Rock" begins, "Gentlemen / One year over there / An you'll age ten." It is the standard Vietnam speech, in the dismal stock cadences of the career NCO, the lifer. Then it goes on to ask for verification, makes its own rhetorical challenge: "Am I exaggeratin' Sergeant Rock? / You ask Sergeant Rock / If I'm exaggeratin." For Sergeant Rock is indeed the authority: "Sergeant Rock was in the army / Since the day he was born," the poem concludes; "He was in the war of the babies."

Suddenly, at the end, there comes the startling, grotesque figure, as if the poem has somehow stumbled across its own terrible truth. Vietnam, the army, an America of scared draftees nurtured on the garish, comic-book exploits of Sergeant Rock and his Howling Commandos: it is all "the war of the babies." The achievement of the poem lies in its capacity to combine a sense of the utter literal truthfulness of that line with an immense power of imaginative suggestion as well. In a single moment it summons up visions of the dying children of Vietnam even as it reaches out in broader mythic terms to embrace a whole generation of Americans, equally "children" of their age, equally born to kill and die as its sacrificial victims.

Here was a poetry of terrible, liberating disclosure. It was the kind of poetry appropriate to a war of cartoon-fantasy heroism gone horribly wrong. Or perhaps a war best conceived of as Country Joe and the Fish played to the beat of live ammunition:

> Well come on mothers, throughout the land
> Pack your boys off to Vietnam.
> Come on fathers don't hesitate,
> Send him out before it's too late
> Be the first one on your block
> To have your boy come home in a box.

Even as "the war of the babies" ground on, the work of literary sense-making had already begun; and it would continue in the prophetic image cast by early writers who had come to see the literary process in conscious terms as a complex heuristic, a way of finding out things, startling and ugly as they would no doubt be, with regard to an experience that from the outset had promised to be peculiarly resistant to signification. The main shape the endeavor would take, of course, would be yet another version of the writer's traditional attempt, to use Frank Kermode's terms, to mediate "the tension or dissonance between paradigmatic form and contingent reality."[32] Often, however, with regard to the particular experience of Vietnam, that "tension" or "dissonance" would be so exaggerated—except in those frequent instances, to be sure, when things were going just the other way around, when form and reality seemed so hopelessly mixed as to make the very idea of "tension" or "dissonance" some kind of grotesque joke—that inevitably the great theme of the literature of the war would have to become the process of meaning-making itself. In its moments of fullest achievement, it would quite literally "create"—often, and in great measure, recalling the sense of high self-conscious artifice that has characterized so much of classic American writing as well—a Vietnam more real than reality, an imaging of what happened there born equally of experiential fact and shared visionary myth, of memory at once forever fixed yet also transformed and illuminated as never before through new possibilities of imaginative invention.

4.

In the Middle Range, 1970–1975

A tour of Nam is twelve months; it is like a law of nature. The medics, though, stay on the line only seven months. It is not due to the good will of the Army, but to their discovery that seven months is about all these kids can take. After that they start getting freaky, cutting down on their own water and food so they can carry more medical supplies; stealing plasma bottles and walking around on patrol with five or six pounds of glass in their rucksacks; writing parents and friends for medical catalogues so they can buy their own endotracheal tubes; or quite simply refusing to leave their units when their time in the Nam is over.

And so it goes, and the gooks know it. They will drop the point, trying not to kill him but to wound him, to get him screaming so they can get the medic too. He'll come. They know he will.

Ronald J. Glasser, 365 Days

What are we gonna do when we get back? Fuckin hippies, fuckin protestors. Fuckin VFW. Who's gonna understand? Who's gonna give a fuck?

William Pelfrey, The Big V

Vietnam writing in the middle range—literature of the years during which large-scale American involvement had ceased while the war itself ground brutally on—revealed significant movement toward new modes of sense-making, attempts to test out the limits of memory and imagination within a dimension of consciousness that might somehow be made to accommodate the extreme possibilities of both. The literature itself was extraordinarily wide-ranging and diverse. In one case, for instance, James Park Sloan's *War Games*, a novelist came close for the first time to bringing off a Vietnam metafiction that actually seemed to work. There were also for the first time attempts to write rather conventional "big" novels of the war in the vein of *From Here to Eternity*, *The Naked and the Dead*, or *The Young Lions*. These included Josiah Bunting's *The Lionheads*, Robert Roth's *Sand in the Wind*, William Pelfrey's *The Big V*, and William Turner Huggett's *Body Count*. There also appeared several important collections of short fiction, including Ronald J. Glasser's *365 Days*, Tom Mayer's *Weary Falcon*, and *Free Fire Zone*, anthologized short works by Vietnam veterans published by a collective called First Casualty Press.[1]

The period produced significant advances in memoir and documentary as well. In addition to Joe Haldeman's basically diaristic *War Year*,[2] there came the publication in book form (portions had appeared in periodicals from 1969 onward) of Tim O'Brien's *If I Die in a Combat Zone*,[3] a genuine memoir in the full literary sense of that term, and a work that quickly established itself among Vietnam narratives as an exemplar of the genre. And quickly recognized as being of similar stature among documentary writings on the war was Frances Fitz-gerald's *Fire in the Lake*.[4]

As a final note on narrative literature of the middle range, the appearance should also be mentioned of works dealing with the war's domestic aftermath. There was Robert Jay Lifton's *Home from the War*, a psychological study of returning veterans, and a work, if somewhat polemical in outlook, extremely important in revealing the awesome emotional price levied by the war on the American generation sent to fight it. And a dramatic literary measure of that expense of spirit was also given with unerring precision and veracity in Robert Stone's novel entitled *Dog Soldiers*.[5]

In drama, there continued to be experimentation with problems of craft itself coupled somewhat paradoxically with a tendency to focus on topical aspects of the war in plays such as George Tabori's *Pinkville*, Adrienne Kennedy's *An Evening with Dead Essex*, and Tom Cole's *Medal of Honor Rag*.[6] In a similar vein was H. Wesley Balk's adaptation, *The Dramatization of 365 Days*. Surely the most important development in dramatic literature of the war (and one of the most important developments in Vietnam writing at large) was the production of two plays by David Rabe, *The Basic Training of Pavlo Hummel* and *Sticks and Bones*. These, along with *Streamers* in 1977, would form a body of work so sustained and continuous as to be thought of as a major Vietnam trilogy.[7]

In poetry, a follow-up volume to *Winning Hearts and Minds* was being collected by veterans and would be published on July 4, 1976, under the title *Demilitarized Zones*. More substantial and significant overall, however, were book-length works by individual writers. These included D. C. Berry's *Saigon Cemetery* and John Balaban's *After Our War*.[8]

In sum, Vietnam writing in this transitional period addressed itself mainly to new variations on the theme of sense-making that had emerged from earlier works. Within an ever-enlarging matrix of vision, it continued to seek out the possible dimensions of memory *and* imagination, with attendant experimentation in genre and mode. In life and art alike, it began to fill in the outlines of its own elaborate mythology.

It is a conspicuous awareness of the complex nature of fictions in general, particularly as they apply to an experience already recreating itself in consciousness through various forms of self-engendered "myth," that it accounts for both the considerable achievement and the more than occasional arty oppressiveness of James Park Sloan's novel entitled *War Games.*[9] With regard to the task of sense-making that faces the chronicler of Vietnam, Sloan at least in a theoretical sense is brilliantly suggestive. The book itself is a demonstration of the distance the would-be novelist travels from before-the-fact theorizing on individual response to war and "ancillary issues" (p. 4), as well as speculation about literary precedent, to his eventual emergence on the other side of an experience that in the very moment it has promised to get "real" has instead wound up hopelessly "metaphysical; one might say a platonic form" (p. 144). On the verge of "realizing" itself, "it all smacked of a simulation," he confesses, "that had not come off" (p. 154). The difficulty with the book, especially in the early stages, is that there is too much talk of this sort. It is Vietnam as literary conceit, Vietnam as envisioned by someone well trained in philosophy who seems to have found Kafka and Borges at a particularly impressionable stage in his evolution.

Sloan is unquestionably aware of the perils of his self-conscious stance as metafictionist. Early on, he pricks at his own literary seriousness. "If I can decide which type of book should be written about Vietnam," he says, "I'm sure my book will be the definitive one" (p. 4). And later, when Vietnam has genuinely "happened," when the narrator has gunned down a squad of raping and plundering ARVN rangers he has accompanied on patrol, when he has learned truly of the horror from Rachow, the mad colonel, and black K.C., the war-loving operations sergeant, both dead and broken now, their bodies lying lost in the vastness of the U Minh Forest, he admits that the lessons of experience have engendered new lessons of art. "I am telling of my experiences as they seemed to me," the chastened narrator writes near the end. "Later I shall go back and read between the lines." Yet he knows "it will probably do no good. If I am truly an intellectual, the truth will not be in me" (p. 181).

To "intellectualize" the war, to bring it to terms with some abstract notion of formal articulative design, is in certain measure the writer's unavoidable task. Yet there will always be some reserve of consciousness, Sloan tells us again and again, that must and will resist such intellectualization. Experience must be allowed to tell its own story.

Yet to chance that is to chance having one's whole formal enterprise spin wildly out of control. Indeed, the "real" war often enough turns out to be something an intellectualizer could not catch even if he tried.

The real war lies high above the ground in the wheeling, vertiginous rolls of a gunship, in curses hurled high at night above the scream of the engines and the whacking blades:

We stood in the open doors and shouted challenges a thousand feet down.

"Come on you bastards, mix it up. I paid good money for this goddamn seat. Let's see some punches. Candy asses!"

"Come on, nick me so I can get a Purple Heart."

Our machine guns useless in the dark, we poured a barrage of mucus and urine upon the countryside.

As K.C. unbuttoned his fly, I recalled my childhood wish to see the heavens open and an airliner empty its toilets on the head of the corner cop.

"You mothers that can't swim better head for the sampans." [P. 126]

The real war is also an insane conspiracy, as the narrator comes to realize, of prudential ticket-punchers such as the officer he sees on a bus and recognizes from the news as "a former aide to the Commander U.S. Forces" who once saved "his chief from being photographed in front of an air-conditioner." He also has an earlier claim to distinction: "While a company commander, he called in napalm on his own position. To save face, the Army gave him the Medal of Honor" (p. 185).

For Sloan's protagonist himself, the real war comes to a personal apogee as he is decorated for massacring a squad of his own allies. Has Rachow covered up his act? Does he genuinely believe the narrator is the only survivor of some heroic last stand? Does the truth of anything, the narrator asks us by implication, ever get seen or get told, and if it did, would anyone be able to figure out why it was important? This is the unsettling and bleak conclusion Sloan's novel reaches. As the narrator has once flown toward Vietnam through what has seemed an unending expansion of time, now, on what he sees in contrast as "the shortest day," he turns homeward. "It will be," he observes, "a clinical phenomenon." Going home, "the vets," he writes, imaging his own final pass as a sense-maker, "will comment from time to time, taking out scratch pads and making little globes with their hands. I will be compelled to watch them all the way to San Francisco" (p. 186).

The intense self-consciousness of *War Games*, then, becomes in itself the novel's "content," a testament to the perils of sense-making in an experiential situation that is inherently sense-defeating. The writer's predicament is imaged acutely in the narrator's primary function as "clerk" and his categorization of the combat reports he must file into two basic types: "Monthly and One-of-a-Kind." For the first, he notes complacently, he can "merely change the names and dates" on the "premise . . . that the facts are interchangeable." The others cannot be reckoned with so easily. "They record singularities, innovative mistakes, windfalls, inventions" (pp. 86–87). Well he might find difficulty in such a list. He has just inventoried the nature of his own efforts at sense-making.

It is precisely in this divide between a Vietnam of reports with interchangeable facts and a one-of-a-kind Vietnam requiring some high imaginative grasp of "singularities, innovative mistakes, windfalls, inventions" that more conventional middle-range novelists of the war repeatedly find themselves. Those who succeed best in mastering the problem do so often by experimenting with ways in which new forms of experiential truth-telling can be brought into alliance with various inherited concepts of literary design, concepts at times quite recognizable in their origins. This is decidedly the case, for instance, with Josiah Bunting's *The Lionheads* and Robert Roth's *Sand in the Wind*, both, in the main, successful attempts to write broadly conceived novels of war akin to those of Hemingway, James Jones, Irwin Shaw, and the young Norman Mailer. Similar in intent, yet colored by a kind of distracting John Wayne nostalgia, is William Turner Huggett's *Body Count*. More successful and persuasive, if somewhat less sweeping in its ambition, is William Pelfrey's *The Big V*. Pelfrey's nearest literary ancestor would seem to be Stephen Crane. In it, the gifts of dispassionate observation that made Crane so compelling a reporter of a war he never saw are combined with Pelfrey's own talent for honest, vivid remembrance of a war he no doubt saw much too closely and well.

The feature, besides Bunting's and Roth's comparable gifts for experiential witness, that brings new creative life, so to speak, to the unabashedly "epic" impulse standing at the heart of their narratives, is the self-conscious, indeed almost self-deprecating way in which the two writers both acknowledge and in a manner mock their sense of formal indebtedness. Bunting, for instance, as he describes a briefing at the headquarters of the American division for which the book is named, begins his narrative in the mock-heraldic tones of the pageant dramatist, tones in their stupid, pompous grotesquerie almost goading the reader to wonder (one of the main points of the work) how the troglodytic, intrigue-filled world of the commander's palace can or even should have anything to do with what actually happens to men on a battlefield. In a similar, somewhat ruefully bemused spirit, Roth chooses as a primary center of consciousness a young, well-educated, "philosophical" infantryman named Chalice, in full ironic mockery of his naïveté. He is a "reader" who, upon his arrival in Vietnam, offers to share the library he has brought with him and suggests among other things that a Negro member of his platoon might prefer *Invisible Man* to *The Trial*, benignly unaware that his black brother has recently read both and would prefer the Kafka (p. 36).

At the same time, however, both writers also seriously employ the strategies of their literary predecessors, attempt to make their world of war a microcosm of their America and their age as well. The dimensions of Bunting's view are established in his choice to depict Vietnam in its relation to the lives of three main characters, of widely divergent authority and background: General George Simpson Lemming, the division commander, bloodless, able, ingratiating, a "systems" man willing to do what he has to do, may it involve even a quite literal parade over the bodies of his own troops, to move on up the line toward chief of staff; Colonel George Robertson, a brigade commander, a decent, honest man, reflective, literate (one of his crucial sins is a penchant for reading Trollope—*The Way We Live Now* is the specific text—as he flies point-to-point in his command ship), yet finally made to accept his powerlessness in the face of Lemming's cynical professionalism; and Private Paul Compella, a draftee, dumped inexorably after a middling American youth into the Vietnam army, playing frisbee one afternoon with a new friend in the squad he has just joined, killed the next night in an action undermined from the outset by the politics of higher command.

Similarly, Roth peoples his novel with an array of representative types: the colonel, Nash, awakening to the insane awareness that the destruction of Vietnam is in a sense a master image of the spiritual annihilation of his own people as well; the lieutenant, Kramer, the child of "Victory at Sea" and *Sands of Iwo Jima*, knowing from the start the war is a botch, yet wondering obsessively how he will do, and learning eventually for his pains only some lessons in brutality for which his predecessors, legendary or cinematic, have done nothing to prepare him; the old careerists, crippled, doomed, slightly corrupt, mainly outdated, Gunny Martin (soon to be fragged along with Trippett, the CO) and the rest, who can't get the new picture, can't figure out the ones who are "too smart," have "heads" that "are so full of ideas, they can't even *hear* orders" (p. 374); the tough, violent, yet strangely sane and resolute enlisted men, Childs, Hamilton, Tony 5, Chalice himself, first called

"Prof," but then later "The Sandman," the one that took on "The Phantom Blooker"—a GI turncoat armed with a U.S. grenade launcher—and "put him to sleep" once and for all (p. 426).

Yet in both cases, for all their clearly "novelistic" paraphernalia, these books also in terms of their sense of vivid experiential authority are persuasively the work of insiders. Bunting sees and speaks as the experienced reader of unit orders, staff studies, after-action reports. His style incorporates the jargon of the professional "hard chargers," the "real sharp individuals," the eager battalion commanders who "orchestrate forces" and "impact" on the enemy. He knows the NCO, bellowing at "individuals" to "utilize" their "entrenching tools"—in plain English, "dig." He understands the enlisted man, lying in a surgical ward with his knee blown off, waiting for a general to make his rounds ("Where you from, son? Real fine. Outstanding. We're real proud of you."), and finally, as the door closes, giving a muttered valedictory: "fucking prick" (p. 188).

Roth's ear is similarly exact, his narrative almost a linear transcription of some insider's code. His marines, in a strange updating of the trench warriors of a half-century earlier who once named muddy intersections "Soho" or "Charing Cross," are now veterans of "the Arizona," the guardians of "Liberty Bridge," the ambushers of "Ladybird Park." They know the enemy, know themselves, speak clearly of these things and the sense of the odds that are gradually wearing them down. There is that part of the odds, for instance, to cite Tony 5, involving the NVA, who are "hard core, like us," he says. "They're just a bunch of slant-eyed marines. You know how they tried to make us in boot camp? Well that's how the NVA are—hard-core motherfuckers. . . . They know how to stand up and die" (p. 329).

In striking new affiliations between experiential and literary values, both writers finally succeed in allowing the war to create, after a fashion, its own master iconography. In a crucial, arresting late scene of *The Lionheads*, for example, as Lemming, half a world away, is decorated and prepared for higher command, and Robertson is quietly shunted into early retirement, Paul Compella's aging high-school principal stands by a graveside in Torrington, Connecticut, his hoarse, high-pitched cry breaking over the anguished questions that the gathered mourners cannot move away from quickly enough to evade: "For what? For what?" he croaks. "This hideous war. . . . Is there a purpose? . . . What did he die for? For nothing? What did he do?" (pp. 202–3).

A similar sense of terrible crystallization is central to scenes in Roth's work, such as the very last, in which a wounded platoon leader rides away from the battle for Hue and catches sight momentarily of a little girl in a bright burgundy dress. "She had a smile on her face," the narrator tells us, "and she waved to him—to a strange man with a gun riding a truck filled with corpses." In the juxtaposition, and the lieutenant's final reflection that "It's always the children that come out first after the rain" (p. 498), somehow the picture has been made complete, complete in all its commingled humanity and loss.

William Pelfrey's ambitions in *The Big V* are somewhat more modest than Bunting's or Roth's, but his picture is no less complete in terms experiential *or* literary. The story of the novel is simple and familiar. It is a tale of initiation, in this case of Henry Winstead, an enlisted artillery observer, and an account of his growth of comradeship with another FO named Fi Bait and his radio operator, known throughout the book simply as "the Anachronism." The three are "college boys," the most unwilling of Vietnam warriors who band together to make the best of it, whose attitude toward their army and their war expresses itself in a series of acts and utterances that often fix themselves into consciousness like a set of master symbols for a whole war-harrowed generation. There is something as simple as Winstead's reply, just out of earshot, to an NCO's suggestion that his hair needs cutting, spoken mainly for his own peace of mind, but also meant to send a message to his army and his America. "I *might* get a haircut, first sergeant," he says, "but I fucking *doubt* it" (p. 97). There is Fi Bait's last radio transmission after he has been denied a retaliatory strike against mortars firing at his patrol from a "friendly" village. "God damn it they're killin us!," he has screamed. "Give me a battery six HE. Give me a goddamned arc light." Suddenly, it is too late. "This is seven-three-seven, kiss my ass lifer," he says. "Negative further, out" (p. 60). There is the inscription, finally, on the Anachronism's lighter: "WHEN I DIE BURY ME FACE DOWN, SO THE WHOLE WORLD CAN KISS MY ASS." "There it is, Henry," he says. "There it fuckin *is*" (pp. 45–46).

Imaged in everyday action and common speech, the experience of the war for Winstead and his compatriots ultimately takes on a sense of compelling representativeness as well. It is mainly a matter of getting tough, getting close, learning not to mourn what cannot be gotten back, cultivating a stern self-discipline, an inviolable irreverence, and an ability just to walk away from it finally when it has gotten too close and there is nothing else left to do. "I guess in the movies the college guy is supposed to be 'the sensitive person,'" Winstead says. "Fuck the movies. I don't want any hassle. I don't know, but sometimes you brood and really do feel like an animal, but what the *fuck*?" (p. 127).

It is a line, like some others ("There it is"; "Sorry 'bout that"; "Sin loi, gook") that in its way can crystallize the whole experience of the war for anyone who carries its memory, the topic of a million radio zingers from the DMZ to the Delta: "What the *fuck*, over?" Pelfrey takes the familiar line and makes something of it. He does so with a sure sense of personal witness and also as a conscious literary craftsman dealing in one of the oldest rites of novelistic passage. The initiation of Henry Winstead is finally the real thing in both an individual and in a representative literary sense as well.

Something similar could be said about a good number of individual stories and sketches included in various collections of short fiction that began to come out of the war, works such as *Free Fire Zone*, Tom Mayer's *Weary Falcon*, and Ronald J. Glasser's *365 Days*. The first, although containing a strong narrative of combat by William Pelfrey entitled "Bangalore" and David Huddle's important story "The Interrogation of the Prisoner Bung by Mister Hawkins and Sergeant Tree," is surely, as one might expect of an anthology, the least even and focused of the three. Rather uniformly, on the other hand, Mayer's and Glasser's works—in individual tales such as "Kafka for President" and "A Birth in the Delta" from *Weary Falcon* and "No Fucken Cornflakes" and "Brock" from *365 Days*—reveal the unique serviceability of the shorter fictional modes in coming to terms with the sense of episodic randomness and strange fragmentation that so often seemed to characterize one's vision of the actual experience of the war: a marine Civic Action team outside Danang undone by the loyalty of a proud, stubborn black sergeant to a mistress who turns out to be a VC agent; a second-tour advisor, the hardest of the hard, his tough composure broken once and for all by the vision of a dead woman giving birth, a ghastly miracle of war; two-man ambush teams, back in for breakfast, with their bloody bicycle chains, the prize NVA belt buckles stripped from their victims, their own growing war-madness, grousing like the children they are about cornflakes, nursing the spooky avidity that will send them out the next night; the commander of the long-range reconnaissance patrol, done with one last mission into the north, safe in the rear-area confines of base camp, yet reflexively lunging at a cigarette lighter that suddenly flashes near him in the night. "It's all right," someone finally has to tell him. "There's no one out there any more" (p. 254). In these and other works, the literary possibilities of the short story and the sketch could make it possible for the experience of the war to be comprehended with an almost gemlike hardness and economy.

Much in keeping with the spirit of the more explicitly "fictive" prose works of the middle range of Vietnam writing— particularly in its tough experiential honesty coupled with a sense of commitment to new literary possibilities of truth-telling as well—was a memoir by Tim O'Brien entitled *If I Die in a Combat Zone*. One of the exemplary works of its kind to emerge from the experience (although surely not deserving to be limited in any definition of its accomplishment by categorical treatment according to the strictures of one particular mode), it recalls both in its own profound humanity and its distinctly literary quality of aspiration toward some large and perhaps enduring significance, the depictions of men at war by Whitman, Melville, Crane, and Hemingway; and it stands at the same time, it is not too much to say, in the central tradition American spiritual autobiography as well, the tradition of Edwards and Woolman, of Franklin and Thoreau and Henry Adams.

The most distinctive feature of *If I Die in a Combat Zone* is the author's conscious attempt, without compromising the essential truth of the experience he proposes to describe, to locate that truth of experience within some more or less traditional sense of achieved context, to use the literary process as a way of investing individual conduct and belief with what may still remain of older ideas of human representativeness and centrality. The account of a young infantryman's passage through a year at war becomes at the same time an odyssey through a whole inherited body of cultural myth, with a perpetual striking of connections, more or less as they are found, along the way; apace, precisely through this synthesizing function of consciousness, the process of narration becomes itself the source of what might be thought of as new permutations of usable myth as well. More than anything else, finally, a sustained meditation not only on the experience of the war but also on the very idea of sense-making itself, *If I Die in a Combat Zone* genuinely succeeds a good deal of the time in quite literally inventing its own context of vision, and in the process it makes Vietnam signify in ways that would set the example for many of the most important works to come.

The task, not surprisingly, leads most often to a method of insight and disclosure perhaps best described in poetic terms rather than those more generally associated with the standard conventions of narrative. Here is no plot, no "growth of character" along some continuous line of evolution. Instead, the book is something like a series of linked epiphanies, a set of meanings both in themselves and in their various possibilities of significant relationship admittedly provisional at best. None of O'Brien's attempts at sense-making connection, old or new, comes off smoothly or easily, or without more than a few false starts and, for that matter, missed endings as well.

There was above all the attempt to come to terms with the idea of personal courage—the familiar currency of modern soldier-memoir, to be sure—but now considered in terms of what seemed an *altogether* misbegotten war, a war more misbegotten in its strange, self-perpetuating agony and horror than anything Crane, Hemingway, or Mailer, one suspects, might have ever dreamed of. By whose definition of heroism, O'Brien asks, were the Americans of Vietnam to be measured? The men who proved brave in the old way on the battlefield, who could actually mount a charge or make a last rush to save a buddy? The ones who kept their heads down and somehow survived? The ones who got medical profiles, or re-upped for new assignments, or kissed officer or NCO ass for rear-echelon jobs? The ones who went to Sweden or Canada or even jail? Or the ones who were smart or rich or just plain lucky enough to stay out of it all in the first place? Although all these questions are implicit in O'Brien's inquiry into the matter of heroism, the only instance of the problem, he realizes, that may allow for some significant possibility of relation between thought and actual experience is the one occupying his own consciousness. There will be his true locus of vision.

He begins to try out connections. He contemplates in thought the austere beauty of Plato's *Laches*. He looks for some experiential correlative in the quiet, unassuming strength of a favorite company commander. Somewhere in between he inventories the sundry attributes of "make-believe" exemplars such as "Alan Ladd of *Shane*, Captain Vere, Humphrey Bogart as the proprietor of Cafe d'Americain, Frederic Henry. Especially Frederic Henry" (p. 142).

In attempting to image the possibility of heroism, he has hardly, it strikes him, been the victim of much before-the-fact idealization—although he is sufficiently a product of his culture to mention early in the text his sympathy for "gentle, guileless Ichabod Crane" (p. 92), and hence betray his youthful blindness to a streak of native mean that he would soon find in his own American soul as well. For the most part, however, the heroes he has chosen from the domain of collective myth, he says, are all figures who had "been out long enough to know; experienced and wise." And each, moreover, had "*thought* about courage, *cared* about being brave, at least enough to talk about it and wonder to others about it" (p. 144). So, in life, the company commander, Johansen, a young, articulate captain, reflective and self-critical, yet carrying himself in battle with calm, resolute grace, seems much of their breed. Like them, he is an isolato, his exemplariness at once his gift and his burden. "He was like Vere, Bogie, Shane, and Frederic Henry, companionless among herds of other men, men lesser than he, but still sad and haunted that he was not perfect" (p. 144).

What is it? He keeps pushing the question back and forth across the reach of consciousness, from thought into action, and then again from action into thought. "The idea is manliness, crudely personified," he hypothesizes, something more than Hemingway and "grace under pressure" (p. 146). Or perhaps Plato is right after all: "Proper courage is wise courage. It's acting wisely, acting wisely when fear would have a man act otherwise. It is the endurance of the soul despite the fear, wisely" (p. 137).

If it is a thing of "the soul," where does it end, and where does plain animal savagery begin? O'Brien talks briefly of Pinkville, of what made William Calley, a platoon leader in his battalion a little more than a year earlier, brand his name and the name of the village on historical memory in a way no other incident or event in the war ever would. He talks about frustration, about rancor, about a blind lashing-out akin to a wounded serpent's recoilings against its own body. "It was good to walk from Pinkville and see fire behind Alpha Company," he confesses at one point. "It was good just as pure hate was good" (p. 121).

Where does "courage" fit in with the stupid, drunken bravado of Callicles, the frustrated, mad, over-the-hill major of O'Brien's last days in Vietnam? What strange voice in *his* besotted soul commands him to mount a personal ambush patrol in the middle of the night, taking the hapless O'Brien with him? The next morning, after he has been dragged in and later reprimanded by the battalion commander—and two days before one last fit of righteous frenzy in which he burns down a local whorehouse and is at last banished for good—he is still saying, "All it takes is guts—right, O'Brien?" (p. 201).

As the book finally demonstrates, all of this, alternately grand and hideous, exalted and crazily stupid as it may be, somehow can be put into at least a kind of context, a context supplied by the process of sense-making in its own right. Or, to put it another way, if there is some true heroism that O'Brien finds himself capable of in this course of the book, it is a heroism of consciousness itself, its power to accept the impossibility of finding final meanings for things even as it continues to resist giving in to a bleak alternative vision of pure brute contingency.

To try to put this all together by way of explicit lessons, O'Brien discovers, is to come out with an assemblage of things that in any attempt at literal transcription seem for the most part rather simple and even obvious:

You add things up. You lost a friend to the war, and you gained a friend. You compromised one principle and fulfilled another. You learned, as old men tell it in front of the courthouse, that war is not all bad; it may not make a man of you, but it teaches you that manhood is not something to scoff; some stories of valor are true; dead bodies are heavy, and it's better not to touch them; fear is paralysis, but it is better to be afraid than to move out to die, all limbs functioning and heart thumping and charging and having your chest torn open for all the work; you have to pick the times not to be afraid, but when you are afraid you must hide it to save respect and reputation. You learned that the old men had lives of their own and that they valued them enough to try not to lose them; anyone can die in a war if he tries. [P. 204]

Yet perhaps the obviousness of all this, the nagging sense that it somehow just isn't enough, is just the point. In a book that defines meaning with such persistence in terms of open, unending process, many lessons will remain that can never be so literal, that will have come only by way of confrontation with some increasing knowledge of all the things one may never fully know, one's sense of the profound mystery of human suffering, patience, pain, cruelty, endurance. They will have come through a kind of poetic of vision that in fact defies literal understanding, a haunted sudden insight into experience that comes most often in those moments when sensations of its utter dreamlikeness *and* its intense actuality seem strangely, even irreversibly merged. There has been "The Man at the Well," for instance, the glaucous-eyed village elder, struck across the face by a carton of milk thrown by a mindless GI bully, licking the mingled drafts of milk and blood from his broken mouth, "with the ruins of goodness spread over him," smiling numbly, emptily, and then quietly turning back to his work, finding the next man in the line of soldiers he has been bathing (pp. 102–3); there has been "Mori," the beautiful NVA nurse, spilling her life out on the ground from her ruptured vitals, the war's whole mystery of pain and loss played out in the silent passion of her dying (pp. 115–17); there has been the Vietnam Golgotha of the chapter entitled "The Centurion," three suspected enemy beaten and staked to their trees, O'Brien the sentry keeping vigil of the empire. "I went to the oldest of them," he recalls, "and pulled his gag out and let him drink from my canteen. He didn't look at me. When he was through with his drinking, he opened his mouth wide for me and I tucked the rag inside. Then he opened his eyes and nodded and I patted him on the shoulder" (p. 133).

It is the kind of knowledge embodied in these moments of essentially poetic insight that defines the genuine achievement of *If I Die in a Combat Zone*. They lie at the heart of the book in thematic terms, dead center in O'Brien's experience of the war; and they also come closest to standing at some center of vision in formal terms as well. Experience remembered becomes in the same moment experience made to signify in terms old and new through the transforming power of imaginative myth, experience made in effect a set of notes toward its own master iconography.

A far different kind of inquiry into the relationship between experience and the myth-making process as it affected American understanding of Vietnam, Frances Fitzgerald's *Fire in the Lake* presents itself nonetheless as an arresting complement to *If I Die in a Combat Zone*, establishes in its exploration of Vietnamese religion and culture at large another form of context for the sense of "otherness" than O'Brien and so many of his contemporaries often felt not just in moments of high symbolic insight, but simply in being in Indochina from one day to the next. Why was it so hard to teach the Vietnamese democracy? Why did they seem to respond so listlessly to what should have been liberating notions of human individuation and personal initiative? Why were they always so slow in getting about things? Why did the Saigon government take so long to bring about the smallest changes in leadership or policy? How could the NLF wait so long to achieve its revolutionary ends? Why did the average Vietnamese, whatever his political or military loyalty, seem so willing so much of the time just to hold his place in the cosmos, wait out the way of things—if he was one of those lucky enough to survive—in the midst of near-incomprehensible suffering, destruction, and death?

For most Americans, it was the inability even to begin to know where to address questions like these that always made the war seem crazier than it was already. In places, for instance, where heavy fighting seemed more or less continuous, well-intentioned specialists, believing a village had suffered unnecessarily or too long, would try to resettle the inhabitants, sometimes building them a whole new town, clean, well-constructed, cheery, in prosperous country within reasonable distance. After the big move the fighting would begin again, and soon, in the old village, the old faces would be back. Hazarding mines, booby traps, long-range sweeps, artillery firing harassment and interdiction (H&I), random attack by patrolling aircraft, the old inhabitants would quietly find the road back, dying all the way and then dying some more when they reached the familiar place that was their destination.

For someone who cared to know something about Vietnamese civilization, Fitzgerald tells us with unnerving matter-of-factness, this insanity had a rather sensible rationale. The Americans had not moved a village; they had uprooted a world. It was something called xa. Its closest definition was "the place where people come together to worship the spirits" (p. 10). It was a whole self-contained system, a microcosm not only of earthly culture but also of a whole spiritual world beyond.

A problem like this was but one manifestation of what amounted to a collision of worlds. The American world was one of expansion, progress, mobility; the Vietnamese was one of enclosure, limitation, immobility. To use Fitzgerald's illuminating figures, "Americans live in a society of replaceable parts—in theory anyone can become President or sanitary inspector—but the Vietnamese lived in a society of particular people, all of whom knew each other by their place in the landscape" (p. 10). In contrast to the American notion of social fluidity, central to the Vietnamese idea of being was "social harmony," an imperative so strong as to have even its startling linguistic manifestation in the absence from the language of the pronoun *I*. Self could only be defined in terms of functional association: "When a man speaks of himself, he calls himself 'your brother,' 'your nephew,' 'your teacher,' depending on his relationship to the person he addresses" (p. 23).

What sealed American incomprehension of all this was its utter concreteness. The Vietnamese world-view was not something that could be divided into a set of ideas and the phenomenal evidence of how they might work out in practical activity. It was embedded in the very fiber of being, sublunary and transcendent forged into some seamless whole. "More than a 'religion' in any western sense," Fitzgerald writes, "it was the authority for, and the confirmation of, an entire way of life—an agriculture, a social structure, a political system." So, she continues, even the continguous "supernatural" came off looking most like "one of those strange metaphysical puzzles of Jorge Luis Borges: an entire community imagines another which, though magical and otherworldly, looks, detail for detail, like itself" (p. 14).

The title of the book itself is a measure of the abyss of vision that had to get crossed. Fire in the Lake, the image, in the *I Ching*, of revolution, could only be understood by an American as something like paradox, a logical construct predicated on some abstract notion of its own inherent illogic. For a Vietnamese, in contrast, it was utterly concrete, a thing not subject to intellectual analysis, a reality unto itself.

Most Americans, as Fitzgerald reports, would never know any of this, would never even come close to suspecting that it might be so. As a result, the war would just get crazier and crazier for everyone involved, a whole stupid, violent, entropic horror of crossed and uncomprehended purposes. It would just get crazier and crazier, finally, and they, the Americans, along with it.

The final image offered by Fitzgerald of the Americans in Vietnam is surely the most arresting, the nightmare world of O'Brien and Pelfrey and others viewed through the other end of the experiential telescope, so to speak, and precisely because of that, in its strange sense of poetic inversion, yet something else important added to the increasing stock of master symbols that might in sum eventually suggest the full horror and tragedy of what had taken place. They were, she says, "like an Orwellian army" who "knew everything about military tactics, but nothing about where they were or who the enemy was." As they walked the land, the jungle, the villages, "their buddies were killed by land mines, sniper fire, and mortar attacks, but the enemy remained invisible, not only in the jungle but among the people of the villages—an almost metaphysical enemy who inflicted upon them heat, boredom, terror, and death, and gave them nothing to show for it—no territory taken, no visible signs of progress except the bodies of small yellow men" (p. 370). They were, more than anything else, a lost army of violent souls afoot in a grim, murder-haunted wasteland of their own making.

Still another kind of genuinely new contribution to the literature of the war, Robert Stone's novel entitled *Dog Soldiers*, is a witness to how that war-anger and murderous confusion, as the terrible adventure comes to its end, begin to spill out across the American landscape as well. It tells us what happens when the Orwellian army of lost souls comes back.

Predictably, even as the novel begins, it speaks of the end.[10] Converse, an ex-marine who is now just another Saigon wraith, sits on a park bench off Le Loi. He is a writer, to paraphrase Michael Herr, who went to cover the war and instead wound up letting the war cover him (p. 20). Now he sits and waits, about to pick up three kilos of uncut heroin to smuggle back to the world, deadly stock for a no-win suicide adventure he will take on for the simple doing of it. Suddenly he is confronted with a warning of what is to be in the unlikely person of a widowed American missionary, a prim, almost saintly old woman whose husband has recently been "taken from us," as she sweetly phrases it to Converse, by a VC torture and assassination squad. As they talk, Converse gradually realizes that the woman is altogether mad. The hosts of the air are gathered, and the last battle is at hand, she avers matter-of-factly, concluding the talk with this admonition and a comprehensive sweep of the arms that takes in the whole of Saigon at its lush, ripe, decadent heart. "Satan," she tells Converse, "is very powerful around here." "Yes," Converse replies, "he would be" (p. 9).

For the "dog soldiers" of the work's title, Converse and his accomplice Hicks, it does seem indeed some power of elemental darkness that dictates their part in what is to come. Driven by reasons neither of them can really explain, save for some strange debased sense they both seem to possess of Nietzschean existential will, they undertake an ugly, hopeless scam that will lead them on a surreal odyssey of violence and horror from Saigon to L.A. and beyond to the very edge of America, and will leave a trail of seared, maimed, poisoned bodies that is finally nothing less than an arrow of death pointing the war back to its spiritual heartland.

As they plot, moreover, they both know that the business is probably doomed from the start. When the denouement comes, it will be nasty, its only reward besides probable death the prize of knowledge about what Vietnam has cost them, its purchase on the very depths of their amoral, reckless souls. "You can't blame us too much," Converse says. "We didn't know who we were until we got here. We thought we were something else" (p. 47). Or, as he has said a moment earlier, "Let laughter flee. This is the place where everybody finds out who they are" (p. 56). Each has found that out the hard way: Converse in a massacre where Cambodian troops have been personnel-bombed by Vietnamese planes supposedly flying in their support, so complete and phantasmagorical a slaughter that Converse, in his fear, can only press himself against the earth and weep; Hicks in the Battle of Bob Hope, a suicidal punishment patrol he has been assigned to lead for letting a few marines go see a USO show, a patrol from which no one except himself returns. Here is a place where the idea of "moral objection" in any variety one might be disposed to think about has truly ceased to matter. Converse has gotten past that, he tells us, and come up with the operative motto. "I am afraid," he observes. "Therefore I am" (p. 42).

Soon enough, it all comes home. Hicks, carrying the stash, finds his prearranged meeting with Converse's wife, herself an accomplice, a grim setup, a pipeline straight to a drug netherworld that in its manic horror and pain and violence is a stunning replica of Vietnam itself. There are no distinctions between good guys and bad guys, friends and enemies, accomplices and betrayers. So with Converse, who returns to find his child missing and his wife on the run with Hicks. Soon he is captured, interrogated under torture, and kept hostage on the move by his wife's and Hicks's pursuers, themselves a collection of homicidals, addicts, and assorted sociopaths, corrupt police and rival operators, in league with each other and the minions of even farther reaching "systems" extending into what seem the reaches of a whole, vast, paranoiac universe. Converse has once said of Vietnam to his father-in-law, "Being there fucks up your perspective" (p. 124), but only now he begins to realize, as Hicks has warned him earlier ("It's gone funny in the States" [p. 57], he has said, and Converse has wondered what he has meant), how true it has become of his America as well.

Like the war that has spawned it, the whole business, to use Hicks's phrasing, has become "Uncontrolled Folly" (p. 90). The trail of pursued and pursuing and all the others, victims and accomplices and predators and manipulatory silent architects and strange hangers-on, finally leads to a scene of final upheaval on a forested, rocky mountaintop, a last redoubt on a border landscape just this side of nowhere. It is the site of an old commune abandoned by everyone save a burnt-out German guru, a kind of leftover Kurtz babbling away in his lost imperium, and his son, the boy's spooky precocity at once the wisdom of Shakespeare's and Conrad's fools and now interfused with the grotesque echo of platitudes taught him once by a whole counterculture generation. Here, the misbegotten drama of Vietnam plays itself out one more time; the war that has presided over the book like a foetid stink recapitulates itself in present horror. The dark forest, thick with vines and studded with rocky caves and fissures, its trees strung with wires and lights and speakers and hung with talismanic symbols, becomes the Asian jungle. When the explosions begin, the weaponry is light automatic, punctuated by the crunching thud of grenade launcher. The night lights up and fills with mad sounds of death that mingle with a larger cacophony blaring from hidden loudspeakers.

In a sense, it occurs to Hicks, the war has come full circle.

The dog soldier has become his other, the guerrilla on the run. "I'm the little man in the boonies now" (p. 296), Hicks thinks as he fights his way down the mountain. Dog soldiers they are, one and all. Yet he is still only part way, the American, to the final truth of the experience. That will come later on, as he tries to stagger out, dying of his wounds, across a desert wasteland. In his last moments, as in the times that once inexorably pointed him there, the Zen Walker, the pain carrier is back in the corps, Semper Fi (p. 330).

So it is with Converse, coming away empty handed, on the run with a wife even more harrowed and junk-ridden than she was when he left. He realizes even more explicitly that it all began years earlier in "the Yokasuka geedunk," and that even if then "they had been able to see how everything would end, they would probably have done it all anyway. Fun and games, amor fati. Semper Fi" (p. 337). They have been fated to defend a principle: that nobody ever knows why they do what they do. They just do it. "That's the principle we were defending over there," he tells his wife near the end. "That's why we fought the war" (p. 307). The principle has come home, but it has not changed at all. Dog soldiers: amoral wandering avatars of the Lone Ranger (p. 272), Terry and the Pirates (p. 144), the image of the total American, *l'homme serieux* (p. 270). They have come home, and there has been the horror, waiting to meet them. "Fucking L.A., man," Hicks has said at one point, "—go out for a Sunday spin, you're a short hair from the dawn of creation" (p. 164). It is the horror, all right, and they have gone out to find it only to make the more awful discovery in their coming back of where it has been lodged from the beginning.

In the most important contributions to the dramatic literature of Vietnam during the period 1970–75—David Rabe's *The Basic Training of Pavlo Hummel* and *Sticks and Bones*, the first two plays in what, with the addition of *Streamers* in 1977, would become a major trilogy—the principle of bringing the war home evolved into a central thematic issue. Similarly, as in *Dog Soldiers*, the attempt to explore the effects of Vietnam on actual American life would also come to suggest the degree to which the war's horror had been implicit in the American character from the outset, a collective tragedy waiting to happen, a prophetic curse hiding at the heart of a whole mythology of culture.

The range and ambition of Rabe's endeavors are suggested in the two plays by the large formal challenges he poses for himself. In both *The Basic Training of Pavlo Hummel* and *Sticks and Bones*, he deals in visions of pure hackneyed Americana, opts for the mode of the almost oppressively quotidian and familiar. In the first, he works (as he will again in *Streamers*) the old American ground of boot camp and barracks, the world of *See Here, Private Hargrove* and *Sands of Iwo Jima* and *No Time for Sergeants*, and later on of Ernie Bilko and even Beetle Bailey. In the second, his broad-ranging debts to domestic and popular lore are equally evident. The blinded veteran, David, returns to his family, including Ozzie the father, Harriet the mother, and Rick the younger brother, who hops about with a snapshot camera and asks plenty of vaguely cute, witless questions. At issue in these plays, then, is not only the experience of Vietnam but also the nature of what passes for reality in America, and how the war is precisely the function of a culture holding fast, against a whole accumulation of geopolitical evidence to the contrary, to a sentimental, even banal complacency in some idiot sense of its own goodness and right.

The size of the risk is repaid again and again by the enduring quality of the accomplishment. *Pavlo Hummel* and *Sticks and Bones* bring the war home in all the immediacy of spectacle and even affront that modern drama in its greatest strength can produce. In these plays, like a sore or a boil or an encysted anger that can no longer be kept in, Vietnam spills its hot burden across the whole reach of our collective existence as a people.

Pavlo Hummel is a mad, inexhaustible pastiche of the American experience of Vietnam in the fullness of its commingled banality and terrifying waste. It is a collection of master images. The play opens with Pavlo in a Saigon bar, stinking, foulmouthed, high-school drunk: "Creezy, creezy," his whore says; "Dinky Dow," Pavlo echoes, the little of a pidgin Vietnamese he has learned. Then, like all drunks feeling sorry for themselves in a strange place, he begins to tell the usual sad story, sloppy, stumbling persiflage about lost love and other confidings. Once he and a girl even got a cat, he says, made it a "kitty box, which," he explains solemnly, "is a place for a cat to shit." The whore replies better than she knows. "Talk 'shit.'" she says. "I can talk 'shit.' Numba-ten talk" (p. 8). Appropriately, just as he has begun to spill his guts in a figurative sense, a grenade is thrown into the bar. Pavlo gets his real chance. In an enactment of the worst fear of every GI in the war, he wakes up dead (p. 9).

Afoot on the landscape of death, and accompanied by Ardell, the black comrade who serves as his slangy, irreverent GI Virgil, he now voyages in retrospect through the last stage of the American life that has eventually brought him to his moment of second-rate apotheosis. With him, we get to see the basic training as the *basic* training of Pavlo Hummel, the means whereby he learns, as the author notes, "only that he is lost, not how, why, or even where." If he has time to work up a talent, it is only the one he already has "for leaping into the fire" (p. 110).

From the outset Pavlo is the platoon maggot, the dipshit, the sorry little guy with pimples or a funny name who will go to a gook shop and get a jacket made that says "Born to Kill," or "I'm a Lover, Not a Fighter." He accepts his fate even before it has killed him, never sees how much it is the prize of his own perfect hopelessness:

PAVLO: I gotta go to Vietnam, Mickey.
MICKEY: Vietnam don't even exist.
PAVLO: I gotta go to it.
MICKEY: Arizona, man; that's where you're goin'. Wyoming. [P. 66]

If Pavlo is born of old war movies, as his mother has told him once (p. 75), this time he cannot even get a handle on the ready-made lines. So it would seem with life-or-death stage directions as well. "You gonna see some funny shit, Gen'lman," his old sergeant has once shouted down from his platform. "You gonna see livin' breathin' people disappear. Walkin' talkin' buddies. And you gonna wanna kill and say their name. When you been in so many fights and you come out, you a survivor. It what you are and do. You survive" (p. 97). This is the bottom line in Vietnam, and even it is something Pavlo cannot reach. As in his abortive American life, so in his quick, inglorious American death, he has truly experienced nothing. He wakes up dead in Vietnam just the way he did on the day he was born. "*Place and time: the United States Army, 1965–1967*" (p. 5). Pavlo does not survive. David, in *Sticks and Bones*, has managed it, barely. One wonders what he has achieved in the bargain. He is blind, self-pitying, bitter, guilt-ridden. Yet that, as they would have told him in the army, is a personal problem. As a casualty, we learn quickly, he is but one of many. The sergeant major who delivers him to the family doorstep says, "I've got trucks out there backed up for blocks. Other boys. I got to get on to Chicago, and some of them to Denver and Cleveland, Reno, New Orleans, Boston, Trenton, Watts, Atlanta. And when I get back they'll be layin' all over the grass; layin' there in pieces all over the grass, their backs been broken, their brains jellied, their insides turned into garbage. One-legged boys and no-legged boys. I'm due in Harlem; I got to get to the Bronx and Queens, Cincinnati, Saint Louis, Reading" (pp. 131–32).

David's problem, moreover, albeit the stuff of collective national tragedy, remains largely personal even when he is brought back to "the family home." It is not easy for "the perfectly happy family" in America, the playwright tells us, when a son comes home from Vietnam "no longer lovable" (p. 225).

The household of *Sticks and Bones* is the "image" (p. 225) of that family, so much the image that it is nearly a caricature of itself. Hence the condition of ugly, unreal tension that creates itself when the peevish, maimed, strange-acting David returns from Vietnam, with his talk of Zung, his yellow whore, and of the squalor and suffering he has seen, and forces the people who used to call him son and brother, Ozzie and Harriet and Ricky, to confront the whole American mythology of a happy life on which they depend for their very existence.

The story of the play is the family's attempt to remain ignorant of that challenge. Rabe has said that this work was meant to be a combination of "farce, horror movie, TV situation comedy" (p. 226). Effectively, he runs out the combination in reverse order. The sitcom is the image of happiness that is its own parody; the horror movie is the reality of a war coming home; the farce is the attempt to dodge that reality.

The farce is Ozzie's constant recourse to a wondrous store of platitudes he has always used to clear away the jitters. "The air's been cleared, that's what I mean," he says at one typical point, "—the wounds acknowledged, the healing begun. It's the ones that aren't acknowledged—the ones that aren't talked over—they're the ones that do the deep damage. That's what always happens" (p. 152). What he does not and cannot realize is that he has just told the absolute awful truth of his own situation.

The farce is family snacks, family movies, family horseplay, and family priest, a whole set of clichés marshaled against realities that will not go away: a blind, unlovable lump up in his bedroom; the spectre of his yellow whore just outside the living room archway. When the clichés fail, there are also more desperate measures. Perhaps there is some mistake; perhaps some checking can be done. "We've got somebody living in this house who's killed people," Ozzie tells Harriet, "and that's a fact we've got to face. I mean, I think we ought to do some checking. You know that test where they check teeth against old X-rays" (p. 196). After all, it may not be the right boy—although earlier Ozzie has recalled "a mean . . . foul-tempered little baby" and has admitted to being "glad I was *here* when they sent him off to do his killing" (p. 126). "We're talking about bombs and guns and knives," he now goes on, "and sometimes I don't even think it's David up there. I feel funny . . . sometimes . . . I mean, and I want his fingerprints taken. I think we should have his blood type—" (p. 196).

Things get worse. The trucks come back. David peevishly demands to have them and the new bodies inside too. "I want them all here, all the trucks and bodies. There's room. *(Handing Rick the guitar)* Ricky can sing. We'll stack them along the walls." Then there is Zung, too, the yellow whore. Enough is enough. Ricky smashes the guitar down on David, screaming, "We hate you, goddamn you." To David and Zung Ozzie cries, his hands around the girl's neck in a death-clutch, "I spit on you, the both of you; I piss on you and your eyes and pain. Flesh is lies. You are garbage and filth. You are darkness. I cast you down" (p. 217).

The spectre-presence somehow gone, it is as if a curse has been lifted. "I saw this really funny movie last night," Rick babbles cheerily, "this really . . . funny, funny movie about this young couple and they were going to get a divorce but they didn't. It was really funny" (p. 217). Soon all the talk turns to TV and groceries and what day it is. There is a flurry of tidying up in the living room. Only one problem remains: what to do with David.

Suddenly, the answer is there like some sweet, inescapable revelation. David will quietly commit suicide. It will be a mercy to him. A razor is brought, and towels and silver pans to catch the blood. David, with Ricky's help, cuts his wrists. He grows quiet, weakens. He is told to take off his glasses. He does. The family talks. Ricky gets off a last picture with his Instamatic.

RICK: Mom, I like David like this.
HARRIET: He's happier.
OZZIE: We're all happier. [P. 223]

It is as if nothing has ever happened at all. A living American dream, the "image of how the perfectly happy family should appear" settles back again into the everyday business of being perfectly happy.

"Stylization . . . is the main production problem," Rabe writes in the stage instructions for *Sticks and Bones*: how to achieve form "where form was sought" and still respond to the imperatives of "content" (p. 226). This likewise remains the crucial problem of Vietnam poetry in the middle range, although much of it also reveals some significant progress toward resolving the split so frequently apparent in earlier poems between dogged itemization of particulars on one hand and moral, philosophical, or aesthetic abstraction on the other. This is true, in various ways, of at least three major volumes published between 1970 and 1976, two the work of individual poets—D. C. Berry's *Saigon Cemetery* and John Balaban's *After Our War*—and the other a new anthology entitled *Demilitarized Zones*, from the veterans' collective earlier responsible for *Winning Hearts and Minds*. What these works generally share in increasing measure, like the narrative and dramatic works of the period, is a fundamental organicism, a sense of "speaking in context" that seems frequently to be missing from much earlier writing of all varieties. Again, moreover, this seems to be in large part a function of the Vietnam writer's increasingly complex and sophisticated ability to see consciousness itself as the ground of a new reality somehow born equally of memory and imaginative invention, a Vietnam somehow more true in its achieved signification than anything that had ever existed in fact. The large-scale assimilation of the war to the terms of poetic sense-making had begun in earnest.

As might be expected of almost any book by many hands, *Demilitarized Zones*, of the three works mentioned, is surely the least sustained and even in its reconciliation of experiential and literary perspectives. Yet if there are still certain instances of a plodding concreteness facing off against various kinds of strained or obtrusive invention, most of the poems do make considerable movement toward an "organic" or "inevitable" sense of mediating perspective. Indeed, two in particular come close to making that idea of mediation itself their collective raison d'être, so to speak. Not surprisingly, they turn out to be among the strongest in the volume.

The first, "Rice Will Grow Again," by Frank A. Cross, Jr.,

concerns a soldier's memory of a friend named Mitch who has
come upon a farmer planting rice and for no particular reason—or perhaps for a lot of particular reasons—fear, frustration, anger, suspicion, the power of nervous reflex, the idea of
the "dud rounds" that have had him "steppin light" all day—
has suddenly "ripped the farmer up the middle / with a burst of
sixteen." As the patrol begins to move on, the poet recalls,

> I saw rice shoots
> Still clutched in one hand.
> He bubbled strange words
> Through the blood
> In his mouth.
> Bong, the scout,
> Told us the farmer
> Said:
>
> "Damn you
> The Ricewill
> Grow again!"

The poet thus far has summoned up a transpiercing personal
vision of pain and waste. There is also more to the poem, however, and it is singularly important. In addition, there is now
the attempt to bring memory home, to place it in something
like a context of collective vision as well. "Sometimes," the
narrator tells us in conclusion,

> On dark nights
> In Kansas,
> The farmer comes to
> Mitch's bed;

> And plants rice shoots
> all around.

It is a crucial step toward meaning, this attempt by the poet in some new imaginative dimension of consciousness to see whatever it is Mitch still sees, and to have us see as well, to share a vision of what that old experience has become now, years later, on dark nights in the heart of America. Memory has been transformed into a haunted dream that is our common possession.

The idea of memory transformed through some new power of imaginative insight into a means of both individual and collective sense-making is similarly at issue in Perry Oldham's "War Stories," a poem so seemingly different from "Rice Will Grow Again" in tone and perspective as to demonstrate in itself how central this recurrent conception of literary process was becoming for Vietnam poetry at large. It is not nearly so savage as Cross's poem. If anything, it is quite funny. That is just the point. Operating now in the more or less objective, and in this case ironic dimension of consciousness itself, Vietnam poetry *could* be funny and still summon up a collective dream of horror like a grim bottom chord:

> Have you heard Howard's tape?
> You won't believe it:
> He recorded the last mortar attack.
> The folks at home have never heard a real
> Mortar attack
> And he wants to let them know
> Exactly
> What it's like.

> Every night he pops popcorn
> And drinks Dr. Pepper
> And narrates the tape:
>> Ka-blooie!
>> Thirty-seven rounds of eighty millimeter—
>> You can count them if you slow down the tape.
>> There's an AK.
>> Those are hand grenades.
>> Here's where the Cobras come in
>> And whomp their ass.

Here is "memory" indeed, memory as literally conceived as it could possibly be, combat reduced to a cassette recording. Howard, the shortround, the basic-issue dufus, looks forward to coming home. He sends his war ahead on tape. Full of some idiot notion of high drama, at once comic and terrible, he "narrates" the war. He wants "the folks at home" to find out "exactly / What it's like." For all Howard's wondrous foolishness, the kind of foolishness, probably, that only an American could come up with, this is what still finally commands our sympathetic understanding of the pathetic voice-over travesty he acts out: his commitment to at least an intuitive sense of the possibility—even one he may have to stage or invent—of opening up some as yet unexplored dimension of collective sense-making. And at one ironic remove, his failure becomes the poem's success, the imaging of a need for common signification that is both his and ours.

For D. C. Berry in *Saigon Cemetery* (and, as will presently be seen, for John Balaban in *After Our War* as well), a comparable sense of the need both to preserve and fix the experiential memory of Vietnam in all its terrible immediacy and at the same time to suggest its new possibilities of meaning within some larger, imaginative context of vision common to us all, is central, and even architectonic. On the side of memory, for instance, Berry's book goes beyond the rendition of particulars to get, so to speak, at the experience beneath the experience—to get inside the numb terror, in one exemplary case, of a soldier "lungshot in a rice / paddy" and make that soldier "you," let "you" know how it feels to drown

> in your own unhomeostatic
> globules each
> Time
> you swallow a pail
> of air pumping like you
> were
> bailing out the whole
> world.

So it is also with booby traps, no longer just something new for the vocabulary, but now something the reader knows and feels, one more step of his own toward the GI's vision of death:

> The way popcorn   pops   is
> the way punji sticks snap
> into your skin and stab
>
> pricking urine
> into   cardiovascular
> systems and apparatus
> apparently
> unorganizing then demonstrating
> it
>
>   then you die

either from the spike,
the   p,
or the

sun gone to grain
expanding

in your eye.

If not the booby traps, then the bullets, Berry goes on. This is
how it looks, sounds, feels:

This is the end where the begin
ning starts with the zing
   ing   unacrobatic
        bullet

that knows
that it is more

absolute

Algebra than Calculus

nevertheless
northemore

it knows
            that when the wind
stops blowing by it

that it
is at

        the end

where

absolute
zero

begins
to
begin.

As an attempt to commit Vietnam to terms of collective vision, all this would seem so far, as I have suggested, to be something like an attempt to out-experience experience, to find some null point of the utterly concrete. Yet as even the typography of the poems reveals, Berry's concept of overall literary design, like his notion of immediate sensory truth and how it gets constituted, is bound up with a decidedly experimental sense of aesthetic invention, one at times even obtrusively so. The jumpy spacing, the short metrical phrases, the elliptical syntax, the erratic and nervous shifting from line to line and margin to margin—all these literary strategems are obviously (at times too obviously) meant to stand in some new creative dimension as formal correlatives to the character of the actuality the poet is trying to describe.

Neither is Berry afraid to admit an unabashed "aesthetic" interest in connecting up his private witness-bearing with more expansive visions of collective myth. Many of the poems are explicitly art poems, acknowledging the traditions of literary sense-making within which they stand. He summons up sources of influence, wanted and unwanted. "Go catch a falling burningstar," he begins one poem,

and give it to the Vietnamese Piers
Plowman peasant in the eternal
paddy kneedeep . . .

>   he notices with an antique eye soft
>   as strange glass . . . .

"Miss Flannery O'Connor," he writes, somewhat closer to home,

>   I
>   went down
>   down to Saigon cemetery
>   and
>   found you sitting
>   as usual
>   casual about death.

"Dr. Zhivago," he asks,

>   could I invite you in
>   for a toast
>   of blood and phlegm—
>
>   if you don't
>   like its   ungray/red   color
>   butter
>   it yellow.

In "Flannery O'Connor," where he proceeds on to something curiously like a new, mock version of "The Anecdote of the Jar"—

>   Empty fruit jars
>   strewn about.

> Not your jars they say,
> for you had only a
> dark jar
> and there are several clear
> Masons here.

—and in another poem where he describes a protagonist named "Sgt. Sam Sublime"—

> Sgt. Sam Sublime never died
> when he was killed cause he kept
> his heart in a blue
> guitar.

—Berry would also seem to invoke the literary shade of Wallace Stevens. Yet in his recurrent insistence on the utter "thingness" of experience, and the essential organicism of its relationship to the process of poetic sense-making, he would also seem equally the heir of William Carlos Williams or Walt Whitman.

Berry also notes and acknowledges the connection of his meditations with forms and processes associated with myth-making of a far more pedestrian sort. "If I'm zapped," he proposes matter-of-factly,

> bury me
> with a
> comicbook   let
>
> Tennyson keep his
> buried William Shakespeare   put

<pre>
     a comic
     on my   chest   and   shovel
     me   overtight

          in my new life I'll be

     Clark Kent

     instead
     of

     Superman.
</pre>

And so with another culture-hero as well:

<pre>
     At Dak To Casey Jones
     was killed in a gunship
     which in a hurry he let whirr
     hot-throttle into Hill 919.
     Remembering the rust on the
     Rock Island Line boxcars,
     he wished he could rust,
     rust rather than rot, to rust
     and rest in the iron tracks
     and not be turned indiscriminantly
     by an easy
     worm.
</pre>

The most important source of influence for the book as a whole, however—the work of a figure whose writing has itself wound up suspended a good deal of the time, appropriately, between the realms of high art and popular myth—does not get mentioned explicitly *or* by way of allusion. Nonetheless, evidence of E. E. Cummings's dominion (with perhaps a small nod in the direction of Emily Dickinson) fills the book. Berry's fractured colloquialism, his studied avoidance of punctuation, his preference for the lower case, his eccentric experiments in word placement and the spacing of individual lines and stanzas: all of these things bespeak his indebtedness to that figure who was himself the survivor of yet another lost generation's war. So in general does Berry's persistent straining to be "hard" about things, his combination of dutiful grim truth-telling with what is at times a kind of rueful gaiety, almost an apology that he has to sound so bitter.

Saigon Cemetery ends on a note of possibility, however, possibility that serviceable meaning can be made, the memory of things at least at times assimilated into common imaginative terms that consciousness can bear. The result, Berry says, will be "salt lick" poetry, not "sugar candy." It will be poetry made "a preservative." It will be sturdy, staunch,

> Something to make a tongue
> tough enough to taste
> the full flavor
> of beauty and grief.

Through the course of his book, Berry tries to render the authentic character of the experience of Vietnam while seeming to let the process of its imaginative unfolding into larger dimensions of art and collective myth come more or less as it may. Far more concentrated in both the substance and manner of its striving after such connections is John Balaban's *After Our War*. The latter work is an attempt to put Vietnam "in context" in the largest sense of that expression, to project memory into creative union with the sense of high and fully achieved imaginative comprehension that has traditionally marked the major art of a given age.

The key term in the process for Balaban—although he never uses it outright—is something like *culture*[11] as writers such as Ezra Pound and T. S. Eliot seem to have commonly conceived of the term in the years just following "their" war. Balaban's book, like many of the works of these distinguished predecessors, is an unabashed attempt to recreate the function of culture as a sustaining matrix of vision, a medium of understanding that may still restore us to whatever is left of a sense of whole relation to the world, a context of common human value and meaning.

Throughout *After Our War*, Eliot and Pound would also seem to be our primary guides in many more specific ways as well. There is Balaban's technical virtuosity and range of allusion, along with his willingness to use topical materials and experiment with various forms of popular idiom. There are his translations from Vietnamese folk poetry, his imitations of the Greek and Roman classics, his borrowings from Anglo-Saxon. In these things Balaban reminds us of the Eliot of "Prufrock" and "Gerontion" and later of *The Waste Land* and "The Hollow Men," and equally of the Pound of "Mauberly" and "Homage to Sextus Propertius," the translator-poet of "The Seafarer" or "The River Merchant's Wife," the culture-hero about to set forth on the labors of *The Cantos*. With regard to both writers, however, Balaban's debts are far more than simple homage. They constitute affirmations of a grand purpose, a purpose finally not unlike that, one suspects, of all true poets of experience after all our wars—somehow to put the world back together again, to keep faith with the claims of memory and yet attest also to the creative resilience of consciousness and its capacity for self-renewal in the face once more of some old encroaching prospect of our collective ruin.

This magnitude of purpose is more than evident in the title poem, with which the work begins. Fully entitled, "Carcanet: After Our War," it is accompanied by an epigraph from Thomas Nashe in *Christ's Teares over Jerusalem*: "For they Carcanets of Pearle, shalt thou have Carcanets of Spyders, or the Greene Venomous Flye, Cantharides." So even before the poem is rightly begun there has been established, in terms at once ancient and new, a context of loss, of inversion of meaning and value. A carcanet, originally a garland or decorative necklace, a token of honor and high estate, becomes, more in line with its modern meaning, a prisoner's yoke. This is no victor's laurel, but a ghastly, vile prize of defeat, an ornament fitting for wear by the broken, vanquished agents of ruin in a time of divine wrath. What sort of garland does one wear after our war? Of spiders, or of the poisonous Cantharis, the Spanish Fly of a thousand scabrous stories? Or of perhaps better the "daisy chain" suggested at the poem's conclusion—"This necklace. For you," plaited by "all the old folks—Slit Eye / and Spilled Guts, Fried Face and little Missy Stumps." It is a daisy chain, Vietnam version, a garland of disfigurement and death, a sweet line for a booby trap, around one's neck a linked continuum of explosions.

Thus the world of the poem, a world of the maimed, the blasted, the dead. This is true in terms of physical experience and also, as we learn from the outset, in spiritual terms as well. "When we blighted the fields," the poet begins,

> the harvests replied:
> "You have blighted your flesh." Muck-marrowed,

> bones ungluing like book paste; nerve hems
> shredded or grimed in something foul, leaking,
> we visit each other like a plague. Kiss-Kiss.

It is a world both literally and metaphorically too awful for meaning. "Intelligence is helplessly evil; words lie," the poet complains.

> Morally quits, Hieronymo gnashes off his tongue,
> spits out the liver-lump to a front-row lap,
> but wishes, then to explain; even: to recite poetry.
> Yesterday a pig snouting for truffles uncovered
> moles, blind and bellyful of *Paradise Lost.*
> Gleeful, let us go somewhere to curse God and die.

Here is the failure of all meaning, of all sustaining belief. Hieronymo's mad again indeed.

Kyd's Hieronymo, who became Eliot's Hieronymo, has now become Balaban's Hieronymo, mad again, to be sure, but this time with a dread knowledge that even if he could try to speak of what he has seen, he would be too mutilated to begin. Once there was a Milton, a God, fallen angels, imperfect humanity, but now only "moles, blind and bellyfull of *Paradise Lost.*" Here, the Four Horsemen hold complete dominion. "They had found Home, were Active."

It is a shocking, visceral poem, a ferocious vision of the end. It is one of the few attempts to create an apocalyptic vision of the war that for the most part speaks to us with any real persuasiveness or authority, be it measured in terms experiential *or* aesthetic. For this is not a visitation of fire and sword, but rather, in both its sensory and figurative dimensions, a particularly nasty sort of apocalypse, verminous, miasmic, filth-ridden, altogether stinking and slimy, an apocalypse of flies and spiders and worms and blind rodents burrowing fat-bellied in the earth. It is the song of the bullets, the "Bore Flies." "Every wound has two lips," we are told, "so give us a kiss."

It is a vision of near-insuperable grim waste, a masterpiece of the war's hideousness. Yet if it is as close, perhaps, to a vision of the end as any writer of the war has come, a genuine exemplar of apocalyptic horror, it is also in the same moment, for the book that it introduces, a kind of beginning as well, a tight, harrowed first step on the way back to meaning. Now the poet begins the work that can be found in the war's wake, begins in art to enact the process whereby experience even of so devastating a kind can finally somehow again be imaginatively assimilated to terms of collective sense-making.

Among Balaban's most crucial steps toward such achieved meaning is his gradual discovery, one that becomes the reader's as well as the book unfolds, that Vietnam, "our war," while truly and hideously itself, is also in some degree all wars. If one must keep faith with the truths of experience imprinted by remembering on the private soul, one can at least begin to deal with them by imagining a context in which personal memory might be something like cultural memory, a medium of collective witness and truth. One can make a sense that is at least better than no sense by recognizing the commonality of human experience, and by doing so specifically in terms of that especially rich and complex form of cultural memory that comes as literary tradition. The remembered "worlds" of *Gawain and the Green Knight* and of the *Iliad* can and indeed must be brought into touch with the world of private experiential remembrance, all of them at once casting the light of new meanings on each other. An Old English Riddle, a Vietnamese Folk Lyric, and a Monthly Report on Agriculture from a slain

MACV field worker are vastly different but equally serviceable ways of making essential human meanings, the "stories" we tell, to paraphrase roughly what Joan Didion has said in another context, "in order to live."[12]

Indeed, precisely in the diverse plenitude of such "stories" and in our sense of the infinite possibilities of their connection, we learn that any attempt at meaning is a basic human act, and a preservative one, a rendition, in the poet's own voice, of the song of life. As the poet of *After Our War* observes midway in "Along the Mekong," it is not so much a matter of artifice a good deal of the time as of human attunement, of allowing the magnetic springs of the creative to respond to the pull of the world in the fullness of its teeming actuality. "Why a reporter, or a cook, could write this poem," he says, "if he had learned dictation." Then he continues the thought, much in the vein of another poetic ancestor, Walt Whitman. An experiential hypothesis becomes an imaginative credo: "But what if I said," he goes on,

> simply suggested, that all this blood fleck,
> muscle rot, earth root and earth leaf, scraps
> of glittery scales, fine white grains, fast talk,
> gut grime, crab claws, bright light, sweetest smells
> —Said: a human self; a mirror held up before.

It can all be there insofar as we learn to make it from our own responding. Sense-making, be it that which we inherit or that which we invent, must be given a chance to sustain us after our war. It may even save us for a while. Of the murdered agricultural specialist, a friend senselessly lost, the poet writes, is it possible to say "Gitelson, do-gooder? a fool?" and let it go?

"Am I a Christer and your corpse-monger?" he asks. "Dead I am your father, brother. Dead, we are your son." One must be attentive, even unto the horror, in the hope that perhaps at least something small may yet be made of it in the way of meaning. One must look quickly, bravely, "in the eyes of the dead," get there "before their clouding, before closing." There, "one sees / oneself indeed." Trying to tell the whole story of it may be one of the few ways we have left of acknowledging our collective worth.

In the work's last poem, the mostly terrible business of it all just goes on. Another friend is nearly gone with cancer, another survivor soon to be numbered among the war's dead. In the worst of it, nonetheless, one can still respond to the tug of the human exemplum, and in the very act of remembering find validated some strange intuition of the enduring possibility of meaning in some new, common dimension of the imaginative as well. It is validated in a moment of high insight, at once the gift by some strange transference of vision from one's dying brother yet also uniquely one's own, the common human gift of consciousness in its capacity to ride out the chaos, to resist the eternal dominion of the world:

> Ehrhart, diving and flying in a whirl of methadone
> and realization, watches for star-nesting birds;
> spies a man-bird; beaked, crimson-winged,
> with a body of gold—Garuda,
> who routed the gods, their wheel of blades,
> who severed the snake guard, spat back its poison,
> whose wing-beat rush could stop the world.
> Who spat back the poison. Who dwells in the sun.
>
> Keep moving, friend, and don't look down.

This is the poet's exhortation not only to Ehrhart, but to all the other voices of consciousness that struggle to speak in this book. To the three figures who provide the epigraphs to this last poem: the author of a Vietnamese proverb—"Birds have nests; men have ancestors"; a London newshawker—"Wonderful news today; Cambridge man receives letter bomb"; Elton John—"Rocket man burning up in the highest sky." To Hieronymo in the first poem, without his tongue or his explanation. To a Saigon bargirl who manages, as most of us do at one time or another, to get it all right and all wrong all at once:

> "doy yøúrh/ you miss me/
>   fuck you
>   iwant to fuck yøuø
>
>   i think about you all time
>   you alays in myhá heart
>
> makee love ná
>   make . love . not.. war ....
> fuck....you
>
>   Monique

To Gitelson, who will not settle for an official explanation of an atrocity, who writes, "I'm not satisfied that this is true. I have the following facts and questions in mind." Taken together, these lines and other lines of Balaban's making provide something close to a litany for the age "after our war" as those of Pound's and Eliot's did for the age after theirs. Between "facts" and "questions" they affirm the need for a new synthesis of remembrance and imaginative insight. They comprise the poet's exhortation to himself and also, in sum, to us all.

5.

The New Literature
of Vietnam,
1975 to the Present

I love the little commie bastards, man. I really do. Grunts understand grunts. These are great days we are living bros. We are
jolly green giants, walking the earth with guns. The people we
wasted here today are the finest individuals we will ever know.
When we rotate back to the World, we're gonna miss having
somebody around who's worth shooting. There ought to be a
government for grunts. Grunts could fix the world up. I never
met a grunt I didn't like.

Gustav Hasford, *The Short-Timers*

Well, good luck, the Vietnam verbal tic, even Ocean Eyes, the
third-tour lurp, had remembered to at least say it to me that
night before he went on the job. It came out dry and distant, I
knew he didn't care one way or the other, maybe I admired his
detachment. It was as though other people couldn't stop themselves from saying it, even when they actually meant to express
the opposite wish, like, "Die, motherfucker." . . . It was like telling someone going out in a storm not to get any on him, it was
the same as saying, "Gee, I hope you don't get killed or wounded
or see anything that drives you insane."

Michael Herr, *Dispatches*

The most significant feature of works emerging as part of what might be called the new literature of Vietnam is the collective impression they give of an almost uncanny centrality of sense-making perspective. In them, for all their more than occasional strangeness and difficulty and their seeming diversity of shape and intention, we find the convergence nonetheless of certain recurrent assumptions about experiential truth-telling, literary signification, and their various possibilities of relationship that prove to be nothing less than architectonic. This is true of observer reports such as Michael Herr's *Dispatches*, Gloria Emerson's *Winners and Losers*, and C. D. B. Bryan's *Friendly Fire*; of works of first-person witness such as Philip Caputo's *A Rumor of War* and Ron Kovic's *Born on the Fourth of July*; of novels of combat such as Charles Durden's *No Bugles, No Drums*, Larry Heinemann's *Close Quarters*, Winston Groom's *Better Times Than These*, James Webb's *Fields of Fire*, and Gustav Hasford's *The Short-Timers*; of experimental fictions such as Tim O'Brien's *Going after Cacciato*; of dramas such as David Rabe's *Streamers*, a work completing the Vietnam trilogy begun with *The Basic Training of Pavlo Hummel* and *Sticks and Bones*; and of collections of poems such as Bruce Weigl's *A Romance*.[1]

The "centrality" one senses in these works, I would suggest, is structural in the most primary and far-reaching sense of that term. In significant ways, they can all be considered productively as variations on what might be called a composite or "optative" mode, optative because of the openness and range of its formal eclecticism. Working across conventions of literary genre, it also partakes of formal strategies associated with other media such as film, newspaper and magazine journalism, and television. Frequently an amalgam of literary document, diary, memoir, novel, poem, and play, it is as often equally the product of cinematic montage, investigative report and profile, television newscast, commercial, melodrama, and sitcom. In a single work new journalism may jostle with the drama of the absurd, an advertising jingle with freeze-frame newsreel, *cinéma vérité* with surreal fantasy. As might be expected, it is a mode often not susceptible, finally, to categorization in terms of "fact" or "fiction"; rather, like so much of the most significant contemporary writing, it is designed to encompass both within a new range of sense-making possibility.

Accordingly, the literature of the optative mode is frequently distinguished from much earlier writing on Vietnam by the rather consistent degree to which it successfully combines a near-absolute concreteness—an unrelenting fidelity (fully and vividly realized, for anyone who has known Vietnam) to the experiential particular—with a distinct sense of self-conscious literary contrivance, an awareness (most appropriate to deal with a war persistently calling attention to its own abiding unreality) of the inherent artificiality of sense-making considered in terms of any formal articulative design. A particularly distinctive instance of modern literature's concern on one hand with the "real" or quotidian and, somewhat paradoxically, its concurrent obsession on the other with "form," the nature of literary process itself, as a central thematic issue, the recent writing of Vietnam becomes a classic case of experience finding its own characteristic method of literary representation within the larger context of cultural myth-making as a whole.

To put this another way, the most distinctive feature of the "optative" mode across the whole range of recent Vietnam writing would seem to be the self-reflexive attempt to comprehend what can be known of the war within a dimension of consciousness at once incorporating both memory and invention. Within a single matrix of vision, it becomes both experience imaged forth according to some inherent dynamic of the actual and also experience made to signify in new ways as well through the shaping imperatives of imagination. This is not to suggest that recent Vietnam writing has been largely "metafiction" in the current, fashionable sense of that idea. Most of it is far less flashy, studied, oppressively art-conscious. The dominant impulse of the mode would seem to be something more simple, a basic acceptance of each age's need to examine the nature of its own myth-making processes, to find the crucial nodes, so to speak, where meaning gets made, where even as the shapes of art begin to transform experience into a new medium of signification, experience itself begins to generate new shapes of art in its own image as well.

It is precisely this sense of creative optativeness that defines the achievement of Michael Herr's *Dispatches*, by general consent one of the most fully wrought and authoritative works to emerge from all the literature of Vietnam. Keeping faith with the experience of the war to the degree that the "truth" of it is allowed to seek out its own context, create or invent its own matrix of signification, the book also comes off, however, as a work of complex imaginative ambition, self-conscious artifice of an extremely high order. It finally represents, as one recent critic has noted acutely, "the journey of the author through his own consciousness as he repeatedly makes the journey from innocence to experience in these fragmentary memories, searching for a truth that will be sufficiently central to the experience"; and in the process, increasingly, "Herr makes the necessity of exploring and ordering the events in Vietnam, not the events themselves, his true subject."[2]

One senses the dominant motif of the odyssey through consciousness, the venture into a strange midworld suspended somewhere between "reality" and "art," on Herr's opening page, where he describes an old French map of Indochina that used to hang on his wall in Saigon, a map of nothing less than a lost world. It was a "marvel," he writes, made in Paris, its age and disrepair "laying a kind of veil over the countries it depicted." The map "wasn't real anymore," but even so, he goes on, he understood that it was at least as real as anything else that was being put out. For the kind of reality that could help one tell the story he wanted, like Queequeg's isle of Kokovoko in *Moby-Dick*, was not on a map anywhere, since "true" places never are.[3] Conversely, in Vietnam, one could learn little from even "the most detailed maps"; "reading them was like trying to read the faces of the Vietnamese, and that was like trying to read the wind. We knew that the uses of most information were flexible, different pieces of ground told different stories to different people. We also knew that for years now there had been no country here but the war" (p. 3).

The real terrain of *Dispatches* thus of necessity becomes the terrain of consciousness itself. The kind of cartography practiced here will have to be born in equal measure of experiential memory and aesthetic invention. Only in this matrix of vision will the "information" that Herr adduces as constituting for him the experience of Vietnam (he was, he persistently reminds us, a reporter rather than a combatant) achieve a power to signify in some larger sense of coherent relationship as well. Moreover, in this case it is a matrix supplied not only by personal memory and essentially private strategies of imaginative transformation, but also by a more expansive sense of associative possibility arising from Herr's conscious choice to assume the role of public artificer, his desire to give personal sense-making a representative cultural validity.

Often in the enterprise it seems enough just trying to get on with the first part of the job. In the course of remembrance and literary reconstitution there prove to be repeated instances of high isolated insight that in life and art alike, then and now, could just stop one cold. Although "it was axiomatic," for instance, the author recalls, that the war "was about ideological space," there always came those moments when "you'd stand nailed there in your tracks sometimes, no bearings and none in sight, thinking *Where the fuck am I?*, fallen into some unnatural East-West interface, a California corridor cut and bought and burned deep into Asia, and once we'd done it we couldn't remember what for" (p. 43). In times when one was perhaps luckier, some things could fall out together into a kind of random suspension, Buddhist chimes suddenly mixed up maybe with broadcasts of Armed Forces Radio sermonettes. Only later, though, when the experience had moved through consciousness to a point of achieved context, could come the full, mythic connection, the image of "Holy war, long-nose jihad like a face-off between one god who would hold the coonskin to the wall while we nailed it up, and another whose detachment would see the blood run out for ten generations, if that was how long it took the wheel to go around" (p. 45).

Thus the complex function of creative consciousness in *Dispatches*. It is the ground on which "information," scattered through disparate reaches of time and space, memory and imagination, eventually finds its own ways of connecting up, establishes provisional circuits of sense-making; and it is also a terrain on which one in some cases searches out and in others actually contrives new paths of connection, forges the link between personal witness and larger visions of history and culture.

In this play of consciousness across a range of vision stretching from the realm of essentially factual remembrance all the way over into that of outright imaginative fantasy, Herr is never too proud to take his connections where he can get them. Sometimes they occur in a kind of middle range somewhere between the earlier experience and the forward-moving aesthetic present. "I know a guy," Herr writes late in the book, "who had been a combat medic in the Central Highlands, and two years later he was still sleeping with the lights on. We were walking across 57th Street one afternoon and passed a blind man carrying a sign that read, MY DAYS ARE DARKER THAN YOUR NIGHTS. 'Don't bet on it, man,' the ex-medic said" (p. 245). And as easily, sometimes the connections could also turn out to have been ready-made, complete, even as they got done happening. "Once we fanned out over a little ville that had just been airstruck," he says, "and the words of a song by Wingy Manone that I'd heard when I was a few years old snapped into my head, 'Stop the War, These Cats Is Killing Themselves.' Then we dropped, hovered, settled into purple lz smoke, dozens of children broke from their hootches to run in toward the focus of our landing, the pilot laughing and saying, 'Vietnam, man. Bomb 'em and feed 'em, bomb 'em and feed 'em'" (p. 10).

There were also plenty of things, Herr admits, that, if they could signify at all, even now, at the farthest reach of an attempt at perspective, seemed to hang on mainly just as some kind of weird inside joke. There was the matter of helmet graffiti, for instance: "'Born to Kill' placed in all innocence next to the peace symbol, or 'A sucking chest wound is Nature's way of telling you that you've been in a firefight'" (p. 226). Or a Christmas card from one of the marine survivors of Hue, "a psychotic-art Snoopy in battered jungle fatigues, a cigarette clenched in his teeth, blasting away with an M-16.

'Peace on Earth, Good Will Toward Man,' it read, 'and Best Wishes for a Happy one-Niner-Six-Niner'" (p. 259). What was the difference between *that* example of cartoon logic and the ones that came on for real?—"Guys dressed up in Batman fetishes" (p. 57) ("I saw a whole squad like that," he recalls, "it gave them a kind of dumb esprit"), or "IGOR FROM THE NORTH, every card in his deck an ace of spades," who "wore a sombrero and a serape" and had a face that "went through about as many changes as a rock when a cloud passes over it" (p. 258) ("'Got to go Dong Ha kill more,'" Herr remembers him saying as he gets up to leave). There is the memory of grim wonder that once upon a time anybody could laugh at "a famous story, some reporters asked a door gunner, 'How can you shoot women and children?' and he'd answered, 'It's easy, you just don't lead 'em so much'" (p. 35). There is *Catch-22* come giddily real: "'We're taking fire from the treeline!' 'Where?' 'There!' '*Where?*' 'Over *there!*' 'Over WHERE?' 'Over THERE!'" (p. 210). ("Flynn heard that go on for fifteen minutes once," he remembers; "we made it an epiphany.") Then there was the joke that was perhaps the ugliest of all because it was meant to be so utterly soul-sincere. "How do you feel," he remembers, "when a nineteen-year-old kid tells you from the bottom of his heart that he's gotten too old for this kind of shit?" (p. 16).

In the worst of it, there was the moment that was certain to come of complete inundation, of pure, undifferentiated overload. "I went to cover the war," he confesses at one point, "and the war covered me. An old story, unless you've heard it before" (p. 20). Yet some story, he seems to suggest presently, is better than no story, a good deal better than nothing, at least, to have something to tell. For if "a lot of men found their compassion in this war," he writes, "some found it and couldn't live with it, war-washed shutdown of feeling like who gives a fuck." Others, he goes on, "retreated into positions of hard irony, cynicism, despair, some saw the action and declared for it, only heavy killing could make them feel so alive." Then there were the ones who "just went insane, followed the black-light arrow around the bend and took possession of the madness that had been waiting there in trust for them for eighteen or twenty-five or fifty years" (p. 58).

It is almost as if in some desperate response to the realization of how near he, too, came to being lost, that Herr, in both his private and public capacities as sense-maker, opts to keep working after connections whether they seem possible or not. He speaks for those like himself who eventually found it possible to walk away and for that other army of lost American souls that did not. His title, *Dispatches*, is acute. From the country that was and in some ways still is the war, he sends forth message after message, each going out potentially on one more line of communication, one more filament of meaning that may somehow find its point of context, strike and hold. What defines the importance of the book is how many of these connections, large and small and in-between, *do* get made, do wind up giving us the contextualizing sense of a whole that is altogether much more than any sum of its parts.

This is not to make too much of "structure" in a work composed initially in the form of individual articles and only later presented as a book that can be best described as a kind of serial pastiche. There is a good deal to be said, however, about what does seem to be a genuine architecture of consciousness within which experiential memory persistently undergoes imaginative assimilation into newer and more complex patterns of achieved meaning. One is persistently struck by how the work demands attention to its own sense of ever-enlarging context, how any single observation or datum will eventually be seen to have pointed at once backward and forward to any number of others bearing it some complex relation.

This is true, to choose just one example, of the line that everyone who has talked or written about the book seems greatly fond of quoting: "I think Vietnam is what we had instead of happy childhoods" (p. 244). It has often been repeated, no doubt for what genuinely does seem its almost orphic suggestiveness, altogether out of context, although a good deal of the time for quite the right interpretive reasons. It is an instance of the perils of writing a book in which the attempt to pull out one thing at least seems to imply legitimately bringing all the rest along with it. In fact, in the particular place where it appears, the line has a very specific application: it is Herr's way of summarizing what it was like in Vietnam to be a young correspondent, of describing his comradeship with figures such as the doomed Sean Flynn, son of Captain Blood, and Tim Page, the mad Englishman, "Page, Fucking Page," the war-lover, the "crazy child" (p. 236). Yet in light of what has already come across in the text, it does indeed seem also a quintessentially, almost wondrously American thing to say in larger terms as well. It connects Herr in his chosen role with what he has earlier described as a whole inventory of "Lurps, seals, recondos, Green-Beret Bushmasters, redundant mutilators, heavy rapers, eye-shooters, widow-makers, nametakers, classic essential American types; point men, *isolatos* and outriders like they were programmed in their genes to do it, the first taste made them crazy for it, just like they knew it would" (pp. 34–35). And in turn, he and they seem similarly at one with the rear-echelon warrior housecat living "a fantasy life rich with lurid war-comics adventure, a smudge of closet throatsticker on every morning report, requisition slip, pay voucher, medical profile, information handout and sermon in the entire system" (p. 45). The

seemingly offhand comment in its particular context has summoned up the full accretive authority of the larger one that is
the book itself. Herr, the heavy killers, the fantasy commandos, all become embodiments, to summon up yet another arresting way in which he has phrased a version of the initial
idea, of a terrible "energy," something "American and essentially adolescent." "Happy childhoods" indeed. "If that energy
could have been channeled into anything more than noise,
waste and pain," he tells us in one of the most memorable passages in the book, "it would have lighted up Indochina for a
thousand years" (p. 44).

This is the method of *Dispatches*: the persistent interfluence
of individual meanings into larger patterns of connection. It is
a book that finally both supplies and invents its own context.
Perhaps a more useful figure however, comes from Herr himself, when he suggests that "information" comes to us a good
deal of the time as "Illumination Rounds." The spirit of the
text quite literally impels one to enlarge on the suggestion.
"Illumination Rounds": in attracting the eye to their own self-
consuming, explosive brilliance, they also light up great pieces
of the landscape around, sometimes with an incandescence as
clear as day, other times with a kind of strobe-lit freakishness
somehow even more disturbing than the dark it has momentarily surprised and broken. In a similar way, the light of individual discovery in *Dispatches* often illuminates the landscape
of consciousness at large and with similar results. It locates the
good places and the bad; it opens up those stretches of territory
that can be provisionally reclaimed through the collaborative
work of memory and imagination; it extends itself into the
very province of the "Inscrutable Immutable" (p. 56), putting
its features as well into grim relief, making known at least the
limits of its dominion.

A similar form of "illumination" would also seem to be the object of a second, much-celebrated work of documentary, Gloria Emerson's *Winners and Losers*. Again there is the attempt to master the "information," to move from the telling detail to the creative analogy, the flash of signification that somehow lights up the far reaches of its surroundings. Often in this case, however, illumination takes the form of a self-consuming incandescence, an incandescence fueled, albeit with great justice, by the author's angry self-righteousness.

There is plenty in the book, to be sure, that is not mere polemic. In moments, she quite literally captures the whole war, comprehends it all somehow within a single brilliant image. There is her wondrous understanding of how much of Vietnam could lie, for instance, in Ellsworth Bunker's report, to the *Yale Alumni Magazine*, of old Elis gathering to charter a club at address APO Saigon (pp. 40–41). And there is her vision, in the winter streets of American cities, of "the younger men in surplus Army jackets, some with the patches on them I knew so well: the Americal, the Big Red One, the Screaming Eagle, Tropic Lighting." Did they come from the dead? "For a long time I could not look at those field jackets, always suspecting they had been taken off American corpses in Vietnam, sanitized, pressed and sold as surplus" (p. 9).

There is more to the last passage, however, and it is symptomatic of how *Winners and Losers* often reveals something like a wish to close off the possibilities of sense-making even as it purports to expand them. "The real surplus," she goes on, "was the men who had first worn them and were wasted" (p. 9). The figure cannot be allowed to stand and become in its own right the stuff of new connection. The metaphor has to be pointed off in the way it was meant from the start.

One would be foolish to say that there is something wrong

with caring to write a passionate, angry book about a war that seemed to demand one so badly. What remains troublesome about *Winners and Losers*, nevertheless, is that so much of the time it will not, as *Dispatches*, for instance, almost always does, allow the truth to tell itself, so to speak. Where Herr depicts characters who were, for good or ill, simply what they were and nothing more, Emerson would seem to prefer caricatures—the Commie-hating chaplain, the patriotic judge, the sensitive, draft-resisting expatriate. Where Herr tells the story, Emerson is often too eager to supply the gloss.

Nearly everything Emerson sees, everything she senses and says about the experience of Vietnam, we now know to have been essentially correct. She is "right." The difficulty of *Winners and Losers* even as exposé or polemic is that this "right" or "true" vision of things seems so often to be much more of an imposition than a discovery. What the book tells us seems mainly to be what the author knew from the start. Or, as Emerson herself puts it midway, in response to a sympathetic VA psychologist who talks of her work with young veterans: "She told me nothing that I did not know" (p. 166).

In contrast, growth of consciousness in all the senses of that term—moral, philosophical, aesthetic—seems precisely the point at issue in a third major recent documentary, C. D. B. Bryan's *Friendly Fire*. Indeed, the author's search for a suitable perspective and mode of articulation to come to terms with an Iowa family's loss of a son, killed by his own artillery, quite literally becomes his subject, and the medium whereby he discovers what the war has come to mean for himself and for his America at large.

The lonely tentativeness of that search, and the sense of suffocating, silent irony that would remain, even at its end, are both imaged in the work's title. Less dispassionate and objective than *Dispatches,* equally less a call to impassioned side-taking than *Winners and Losers, Friendly Fire* arrives at its own uniquely achieved vision of what is at once the war's matter-of-fact *and* maddening contradictoriness. If there is information here, the title seems to say, one of the writer's main jobs will have been to unriddle the problem of what that information is.

"Friendly fire." In this case it is the product of Defense Department euphemism. How does one describe in the least painful way possible artillery action in which an army kills its own troops? "Friendly fire." In a world where such expressions can be used by people who actually think their language bears some significant relation to common experience, there is likely to be no right or wrong, good or bad. It will most likely be for the most part just mistaken and shabby and confused.

The difficulty of Bryan's search is likewise reflected in the fractured, almost prismatic structure of the book at large. Beginning with Michael Mullen's departure for Vietnam, it moves briefly through some reports of his early experience and then records his death. Next, it describes the struggle of Michael's parents, Peg and Gene Mullen, with their grief; their confrontation first with the indifference and ineptitude and later with the outright malice and vindictiveness of an entrenched bureaucracy; their growing involvement in antiwar activities; their increasing tendency toward a hard, uncritical singleness of vision finally not unlike that of their presumed adversaries and persecutors; their eventual awareness that somehow the anger would just have to be lived out. Only at this point does Bryan finally describe the incident itself, the death of Michael Mullen, what actually happened as he could piece it together from battle reports, and from the accounts of soldiers who were there, members of Michael's unit. Later he also describes what happened to some of these survivors, how they saw combat, what it eventually did to them. The book ends with a body count and a notation of the exact date on which South Vietnam surrendered.

This, for Bryan, is what can be made of the attempt to come to literary terms with the death in Vietnam, by friendly fire, of Michael Mullen. Like the war, it does not get finished; it just ends. Yet along the way, it has at least taken some important steps toward sense-making, even if only by way of Bryan's increasingly complex understanding of his own authorial task. A clear measure of this enlarged understanding is his attempt—not early but late in the work, it is important to note—to put together one last near-objective version (since it has by now obviously become his point, as in *Billy Budd*, a work remarkable in some of its similarities, that no truly objective account of anything is *ever* possible) of what happened the night Michael Mullen died. Having sifted through the story of it as it has seemed to the U.S. Government, the story of it as it has seemed to Gene and Peg, Michael's parents, and the story of it as it has seemed to arise out of his attempts to mediate between the two, he now does his best to make one more: his own. Now it is enough. If it cannot be finished, it can at least end. "Truth uncompromisingly told," the narrator of Melville's work admonishes us, "will always have its ragged edges."⁴ And it is fitting here, as in *Billy Budd*, that the truth we at last sense most fully is some cumulative truth of art. Michael Mullen was killed in action while serving as a member of the U.S. Army in the Republic of Vietnam. Michael Mullen died in a screwup so miserably stupid that nearly everyone involved felt obliged to cover it up. Michael Mullen died in an accident of war. Michael Mullen died in Vietnam and then died again endlessly in the hearts of his parents in the middle of America. Somehow, out of all that, there has come larger meaning. It is signification still incomplete, but it is surely a good deal more serviceable and even in its way sustaining than any we had before.

The same emphasis on authorial sense-making as complex heuristic process—with similar ramifications as to the suggestion of new possibilities of relationship between experiential truth-telling and "literary" vision—is evident in Philip Caputo's *A Rumor of War* and Ron Kovic's *Born on the Fourth of July*, two recent works of personal memoir much in the vein of Tim O'Brien's *If I Die in a Combat Zone* and even in some ways enlarging on its considerable achievement.[5] Indeed, a measure of the innovative power and importance of both is the degree to which, even as they substantially enlarge the possibilities of the autobiographical mode itself, they also recall strategies of third-person witness employed by Herr, Emerson, and Bryan, and, as will become evident in discussions of books of the past few years such as Charles Durden's *No Bugles, No Drums*, Larry Heinemann's *Close Quarters*, Winston Groom's *Better Times Than These*, Gustav Hasford's *The Short-Timers* —and even Tim O'Brien's highly experimental *Going after Cacciato*—recent advances in novelistic expression as well.

Like most autobiographical narratives that aspire to some larger aesthetic sense of representative truth-telling, be they called memoir or novel or some combination of the two, both *A Rumor of War* and *Born on the Fourth of July* arise from a kind of double consciousness: both writers see themselves as bearing witness to the experience of the war in the dimension of personal memory, and they also present themselves as the chief characters in works of complex literary invention as well. In the two cases at hand, this rather conventional doubling of vision pays some unexpected literary dividends, moreover, since it often turns out to be a rather accurate recapitulation of the actual form of the experience of Vietnam even as it was happening, its terrible immediacy bound up repeatedly with a sense of the artificial, the unreal, even the absurd. To put this more simply, Caputo and Kovic both work in a medium of consciousness that is a near-exact literary correlative to the experience they propose to describe and interpret.

Although of the two works Caputo's seems decidedly the more conventional both in matter and mode, one is also aware from the outset of a sense of extremely self-conscious literariness. Epigraphs from the Bible (including the source of the work's title) and Shakespeare mix with lines from Wilfred Owen and Siegfried Sassoon, Rudyard Kipling and Thomas Hobbes. Within the process of narration itself there is a good deal of complex experiment. There is Caputo's attempt to recapture himself as the young platoon leader increasingly obsessed with his losses, plunged with terrible suddenness into a dream where he leads a formation of the dead and maimed, marching headless and gutshot, stumbling along on their truncated legs, swinging their stumps of arms to the count of cadence (p. 199). There is the recovery of a moment in which he is clubbed to the ground by an exploding mine: apace, some barbed wire nearby strangely becomes an old fence remembered from his childhood, and in the roar of the blast he himself once again becomes a boy frightened by stories a friend has been telling him about bears (p. 280). At certain points, narration at large breaks itself down into freeze-frame stills, visions of war literally flashing by, their passage punctuated only by a series of photographic clicks (pp. 312–13).

The primary accomplishment of *A Rumor of War*, however, the manner in which it brings experiential truth-telling into new and creative forms of relationship with complex literary exploration, is structural in the largest sense of that term. Ex-

perience can signify, the author seems to suggest from the outset, only as it can be seen in the context of a whole evolution of
consciousness. The book becomes an attempt to trace the ever-
changing nature of balance between event and vision, phenomenon and perspective, growth of experience and growth of
mind. The process begins quickly and subtly. Early on, for instance, the boot lieutenant—"Sir, the United States Marines;
since 1775, the most invincible fighting force in the history of
man. Gung Ho! Gung Ho! Gung Ho! Pray for War!" (p. 12)—
seems to be at least somewhat able to stand outside himself, so
to speak, and be aware of the folly of his innocent bravado. Yet
there are other ways in which consciousness has begun to
shape reality that are not so easy to handle. Even before Vietnam, countryside has ceased to be landscape; it is terrain, a
problem for tactical appraisal. In the war zone, green stops
being a color of promise, of expectation. It is now a shade of
despondency—the color of jungle, of paddy water, of soaked fatigue uniforms, of crenellated monotonous rows of low hills, of
a looming forbidden vine-shrouded mountain (p. 98).

Deeper and deeper into war, perception becomes increasingly
a kind of strange exaggerated playing on its own possibilities.
Marines in ponchos, trudging in line across the landscape, become "hunchbacked, penitent monks" (p. 233). Shaving in a
makeshift mirror, Caputo sees himself dead, and, in the moments when he looks deepest, sees not only his own body "but
other people looking at it" (p. 230). A whole battle comes
madly to focus in on a lone VC, "his arms outstretched, in the
pose of a man beseeching God," as he is blown to shreds by a
Skyhawk fighter-bomber streaking across a treeline (p. 298).

On those occasions when it seems it might be possible at
least momentarily to make the war cease, to put it behind, it is
as if reality itself has vanished. On an R&R in Saigon, Caputo

feels himself floating free in a place that is nowhere. Drinking wine and eating cooked food at a table, having bathed and slept solidly for two nights in a row, he can now only think of the utter strangeness of normality (pp. 246–47).

The war becomes its own reality in a philosophical, a moral, and even a strangely aesthetic sense. Eventually it is not a matter of being or consciousness but simply a single overwhelming presence. There is no philosophy, there are no morals, there are no meanings, except as the war creates them from moment to moment on its own imponderable terms. There is staying alive. Finally, there is not even fear. There is something like indifference, a going beyond.[6] In one more firefight on one more afternoon, Caputo just steps over the line, gives in to it all. He walks up and down a clearing, waving his arms, baiting a last, diehard sniper. "HO CHI MINH SUCKS," he screams. "FUCK COMMUNISM. HIT ME CHARLIE." "That stocky little fucker's crazy," he hears one of his marines mutter from a nearby hole (p. 269). The marine is correct. The lieutenant has gone out and claimed the insanity that has been waiting for him. In body and mind alike, he has become the war.

Presently Caputo watches his platoon turn into a frenzied mob as they advance on a run through a village, leaving it, as they emerge on the other side, a pile of ashes, a smoking cauldron of suffering and destruction. It has seemed to happen, he says, in a dream (p. 305). So he feels especially of his own part. It had been a "sensation of watching myself in a movie. One part of me was doing something while the other part watched from a distance, shocked by the things it saw, yet powerless to stop them from happening" (p. 306).

Yet only now comes the truly critical moment. Laughing, almost giddy with war-madness, Caputo authorizes the "capture" of two VC suspects from a nearby village, knowing all the while that what he has really done is authorize their assassination. He lets it happen and finds that one of the two men his troops have killed is the informant who reported the suspects in the first place. All the marines involved are arrested and tried for murder. When one of the men is acquitted, the charges are dropped against the rest. Caputo is reprimanded for a lesser offense, swearing a false statement,[7] and is sent home to be discharged. A botched horror, a dead-end inquiry, a stumbling charade of half-justice: one last fast-action flurry of image and event and Caputo's career at war is over.

The boy lieutenant who once looked with a kind of bemused, tolerant superiority at a sergeant, teaching a chalkboard class in tactics—"AMBUSHES ARE MURDER," he has had his class of grunts chanting with him, "AND MURDER IS FUN" (p. 36)—now realizes that the training-camp caricature has held its own terrible truth. Once there was an English major who liked Dylan Thomas. Now he reads "And Death Shall Have No Dominion" and can think only that Dylan Thomas could not possibly have been in a war (p. 245).

The evolution of consciousness is nearly complete. The younger Caputo who has been the chief character in *A Rumor of War* has become much like the older one who is its narrator. He does not trade in illusions, in bloodthirsty chants, in war stories, in philosophizings, in morals. He will settle for whatever of sense-making can just help him walk away. Yet like Siegfried Sassoon, he remains in great measure the captive of what he has been and done. "Look down and swear by the slain of the War," he, too, seems to hear himself saying, "that you'll never forget" (p. 338).

It is as if in answer to this admonition that Caputo goes back in 1975 as a correspondent who reports the fall of Saigon. "I *had* to see the war end" (p. 340), he says, see through the last debacle. It is not enough for him, he seems to say, that the war has had *an* end, traumatic and well defined as that may have been. It must finally be related also to *the* end, be seen against the backdrop of some larger grim ceremony of public verification.

The account supplies the epilogue to Caputo's book and to his war as well. Again, correlative forms of art and life find their point of creative mutuality. Caputo is there to see "Americans di-di." He climbs aboard one of the last helicopters that lifts off from the tennis courts of MACV Headquarters, Pentagon East. He finds refuge aboard ship with assault troops from the Ninth Marine Expeditionary Brigade—the one he landed with ten years earlier for the "splendid little war" (pp. 211–12) at Danang. Caputo's design of sense-making has come full circle, a book imaged in its own brilliantly ironic final figure.

In terms of structure and narrative method a more explicitly "experimental" book than Caputo's, Ron Kovic's *Born on the Fourth of July* quite literally begins as its author's actual experience of combat comes to an end. Shot through the spine, rescued by a black marine whose face he never sees, Kovic begins the long journey home and the odyssey of consciousness as well whereby he will attempt to come to terms with his own terrible wounds, physical and mental, and also with his sense of the pain and loss the war has wrought upon his nation at large.

The wound itself simply becomes an extension of the experience, carrying Kovic through a train of linked horrors, dogging him to his American doorstep. In Vietnam, still in an evacuation hospital, he wakes up to see a doctor and a corpsman laughing and talking football as they try to cardiac-shock a dying pilot back to life (pp. 10–11). In the corridor of a VA hospital on Long Island, he lines up with all the other wasted bodies to get worked on by Tommy the smiling enema man and then hosed off in a kind of human carwash (pp. 22–27). As the first section of the book ends, Kovic struggles in a therapy room, tries to stand up, vomits his guts out as his mother and sister stand frozen in the doorway (p. 32). The war is still on.

Apace, there come at least the beginnings of a search for a context, an attempt to connect the experience of the war with some idea of a representative American consciousness. There are reminiscences of a childhood, a boy born, of all days to be born, on the fourth of July, reared on celluloid heroes and cartoons, making his first communion wearing a cowboy hat and six-shooters. Quickly there is adolescence, the visit to the high school by the shined-up recruiters, enlistment, boot camp.

At this point, the earlier narrative resumes. There is a parade, Kovic honored along with a childhood friend, now an amputee, blown apart by his own mortars—a parade, it turns out, with a bunch of drunk legionnaires trying to do some good for two messed-up boys from a place that, for all their good will and full hearts and memories of their own wars, they cannot even imagine. There is Kovic's attempt to come to terms with his impotence, a Hemingway conceit come hideously true. There is aimless travel, forlorn daydreaming, drunkenness, a broken marriage, and finally impassioned involvement in Vietnam Veterans against the War, involvement culminating in a "Last Patrol" demonstration against Nixon at the Republican National Convention in Miami.

Even now, however, for all Kovic has told us, there is still the feeling that he has not yet told enough. There is something more that has not come out, some secret of experience unshared and unspoken. There is. Kovic's book, like Caputo's, is finally the attempt of consciousness to undergo something like the expiation of a curse, the exorcising of a hidden horror. In this case, it has been prefigured from the beginning. As Kovic, still in the hospital in Vietnam, begins to go under and give in to anaesthesia, he says to himself, "I think maybe the wound is my punishment for killing the corporal and the children. That now everything is okay and the score evened up" (p. 9). So throughout the book, hints of the dead corporal and the dead children persistently recur, nagging, ghostlike, omnipresent.

Finally, in the last chapters, the whole story gets told. Kovic, on one of his first missions, believes he has accidentally killed one of his own men, a corporal from Georgia, shot him through the throat in the midst of a shameful panic, when an entire marine patrol, after a surprise attack, has run in fear from its adversaries (pp. 173–81). Later, there are the children. A young lieutenant, thinking he has an elusive, notorious squad of VC sappers trapped in a village, moves his troops in for the kill. Someone opens fire early, and the whole line erupts. The patrol rushes forward to find that they have shot up a bunch of children. They are bleeding and dying everywhere, wasted, messed up, blown away (pp. 186–94).

The final mission for Kovic, the one on which he is wounded, he has wanted to see as a chance to make up for these terrible things. It is all "up for grabs" (p. 203), he thinks. He is again losing the bet as the book ends—and this is no literary trick but the author's return to the terrible moment when it happens, but this time with all the truth in—nearly at the sentence before the sentence where it begins. The rounds come slamming home to Kovic's spine. Somehow, memory and imagination drift off together to a Saturday in spring, a kid at the baseball field, "a song called 'Runaway' by a guy named Dell Shannon" echoing across the air, the kid thinking maybe he "could live forever" (pp. 207–8). Kovic's vision of the war, coming back to where it began, has found its context.

As with Caputo's work, Kovic's method throughout *Born on the Fourth of July* is of a piece with his sense of the complex nature of his authorial task. The fractured chronology, free, shifting, reflexive, simulates the motion of consciousness itself, its inquiry into its own processes. Narration shifts back and forth between first person and third in an attempt to give private insight a larger, representative significance. Kovic knows that he is just another crippled snuffy, another body in a VA enema line and hosedown, another angry, aimless, lost vet. But he also stakes a whole sense-making enterprise on the possibility that the telling of his story can also in the same moment be something of a telling of our story. He is also his own master symbol, the culmination in some larger sense of a whole mythology of culture. "I am the living death," he writes in the book's epigraph,

> the memorial day on wheels
> I am your yankee doodle dandy
> your john wayne come home
> your fourth of july firecracker
> exploding in the grave.

He is the new, terrible poem of his America, the icon of a private horror that has now become a public and collective one as well.

If there is a characteristic "structure," some recurrent dynamic of sense-making that similarly unites many of the most important recent novels of the war—works such as Charles Durden's *No Bugles, No Drums*, Larry Heinemann's *Close Quarters*, Winston Groom's *Better Times Than These*, James Webb's *Fields of Fire*, and Gustav Hasford's *The Short-Timers* —it is precisely this movement through consciousness toward confrontation with some vision of horror so arresting in its sense of awful completeness and finality as to possess at once both a terrible individual significance and a kind of iconographic representativeness within the context of American sensibility at large. All of them start out ostensibly as rather conventional narratives of initiation, of the passage from innocence to experience, with the war itself frequently becoming, as has often been the case in our literature, some ultimate crucible of the American soul. They also wind up each telling us a version of what finally seems a single dirty secret at once theirs and our own. It is an echo, perhaps, of what Caputo has learned early on in his war from an aging marine gunny. "Before you leave here, sir," the old NCO tells him, "you're going to learn that one of the most brutal things in the world is your average nineteen-year-old American boy" (p. 137). Or, to put the lesson in terms of a more general applicability: to go "Out There" in Vietnam, "Beyond," is to run the risk of cutting free from whatever it was that once defined humanity and, even worse, perhaps never being able again to get back to it.

To be sure, a giving over of the soul to horror in warfare is not an exclusively American trait. Rather consistently, however, in the novels just mentioned, it supplies an obsessive center. Each of them turns on the need to explore a condition of spirit that might best be described as "the psychology of mean"—not mean in the dictionary sense, mean as in "niggardly," "small," even "base"—but something more like rattlesnake mean, beaten-dog mean. It is the soul's ground zero, so to speak, the place one must go to, they repeatedly seem to tell us, if one is even to begin talking significantly about a war where there was finally nothing to fight for save perhaps some animal sense of numb survival; a war that especially toward the last seemed to go on mainly because no one with any authority had the sense to stop it; a war in which the only real subject of contemplation available became the killing itself.

Or, as Durden's Private Jamie Hawkins puts it in the midst of reflections on the dead of a war that seems a crude combination of "farce" with "some fuckin' far-out reality," there is always, beyond everything else, "the whole business of this bein' for nothin', or next to nothin'" (p. 72). What is brave and what is cowardly? What is purposeful and what is purposeless? These are dumb questions, Hawkins tells us. Why, his platoon leader asks him, has he taken an unnecessary chance, risked himself to save a patrol? "Because I don't want to die out here, you silly sonofabitch," he cries. "Because I'm scared half to death. Because I don't even know why in hell we're out here, five fuckin' people against five thousand pissed-off pig fuckers, for Christ's sake" (p. 263). For those swept up in its manic, almost sublime pointlessness, the war has become that quintessential American thing, "the last word in disposable goods. Soldiers, I mean. Throwaway people" (p. 3).

Phrased more formally, the same set of perceptions supplies a fictitious prologue to James Webb's *Fields of Fire*. Who are the soldiers of Vietnam?, a correspondent inquires of "an anonymous general." And how do they read their place in what Hawkins calls the "mind's-eye" view of it all? (p. 262). "You've met them," the general says. "You know. They are the best we have. But they are not McNamara's sons, or Bundy's. I doubt they're yours. And they know they're at the end of the pipeline. That no one cares. They know" (p. 1).

"Throwaway people," their names at once your basic GI rollcall and the stuff of a high, desperate poetry: Deadeye, Bagger, Short Round, T. H. E. Rock; Crazy Earl, Atevo, Baby Cakes, The Boy Ranger; Flaky, Doc Jay, Snake, Rafter Man; Phony, Spudhead, Ogre, Cannonball, Homicide, Animal Mother. And

the general is correct. They know. "We been abandoned, lieutenant," a young platoon sergeant tells Webb's protagonist. "We
been kicked off the edge of the goddamn cliff. They don't know
how to fight it, and they don't know how to stop fighting it"
(p. 175). Or, as a marine called Chili Vendor puts it in Hasford's
novel, "We're prisoners here. We're prisoners of the war.[8]
They've taken away our freedom and they've given it to the
gooks, but the gooks don't want it. They'd rather be alive than
free" (p. 56). Such is the fate, thinks Heinemann's Philip Dosier, of "a true son of the empire" (p. 53). He is left mainly along
with the others, to return to Jamie Hawkins, with little more
than "a wary look and a badass view of life" (p. 80).

What gets these men through in the land of the mind's
eye?—for invariably, only chance gets them through in the war
itself, and truly does then sometimes when it would perhaps be
the better part of chance to die. In many cases, it is the culti-
vation, in Durden's words, of an "unshakable bad attitude"
(p. 287), a continual exercise of one's inalienable right, even
somewhere out on "the ass-end of insanity" (p. 252), to "say no
to bullshit" (p. 240). It comes out often in a lot of bad talk, bad
talk sounding just close enough to time-honored American
bluster to make one forget that the truth here is probably just
as bad or worse. There is Heinemann's Whiskey J., the ambush
commander, coming back to the wire for a minute before he
heads out, to talk with the MP who rattled the gate: "My man,
we get hit within five hundred meters of this fence, an' I'm
gonna come back here and do you in. If I got to crawl and push
myself along with stumps" (p. 112). There is the Cowboy of
Hasford's Delta One-Five: "Man, we are life takers and heart-
breakers. Just ask for the Lusthog squad, first platoon. We
shoot them full of holes, bro. We fill them full of lead" (p. 34).
There is his squadmate Crazy Earl who loves it, who loves it so

much he will die for it, will die charging a VC position with a BB gun just to see if the thing can be done: "There it is. They call me Crazy Earl. Gooks love me until I blow them away. Then they don't love me anymore" (p. 35). It hides in a look of the eye, a look "not of the trenches," says Heinemann's Deadeye Dosier, "but of the ambush. It is the thousand meter stare cranked down to fifty, to five." It makes people ask later on, "Dosier, you know, you've got the oddest, strangest look in your eyes. Why is that, hey? What have you seen? (pp. 294–95).

Often, if these men sense the commonality of their predicament, see themselves in some brotherhood of death, they also feel a kind of soul-affinity with the men they hunt and kill. Grunts wind up being "closer to Gooks," thinks Webb's Lieutenant Hodges, than they do to the people who make the plans and give the orders that get them killed (p. 136). They get to be at one, Hasford's Corporal Joker decides, with "the shrewd men who fight for survival in the rain forest, hard soldiers, strange diminutive phantoms with iron insides, brass balls, incredible courage, and no scruples at all" (p. 131). The bad guys, says his friend the Cowboy, are something else: "they are hard as slant-eyed drill instructors. They are highly motivated individuals" (p. 73).

All of this, moreover, bad and rough and almost dirty-joke-like as it is, but points us on a darker way. Indeed, as a general rule in these recent novels of the war, when talk is going so ugly as to seem simply unreal, action is generally getting ready to outdo it. As one veteran first sergeant in Groom's novel is finally forced to put it to his young officer, "The truth is, lieutenant, . . . some of these shitheads are getting a little crazy" (p. 270). Finally, as the same work tells us, it is what it turned into in the Ia Drang, "killing for killing's sake" (p. 221). It is what Heinemann's Philip Dosier knows to be "a surrender to cool perfect murder" (p. 294). It is, says Jamie Hawkins, "four or five rounds in the belly. The ultimate argument" (p. 221). It is, for Webb's marines, pure, simple, dead-on matter-of-fact:

> "Ain't nobody can chuck a frag like Phony."
> Phony smiled, chewing a wad of C-ration gum. "Boom-boom."
> Cannonball nodded, grinning, "Boom-boom." [P. 71]

It is a thing even Hasford's crazed, witless Animal Mother can explain with the lucidity of some idiot Solomon: "Yeah, you'd better believe we waste Zipperheads. They waste our bros and we cut them a big piece of payback. And payback is a motherfucker" (p. 136).

"Nobody goes home from here," writes Heinemann's Philip Dosier. "The war works on you until you become part of it, and then you start working on it instead of it working on you, and you get deep-down mean. Not just kidding mean; not movie-style John Wayne mean, you get mean for real" (p. 278). This is America at the end of the pipeline indeed, as Jamie Hawkins sees it as well. "From Valley Forge to Vietnam," he says, "two hundred years to produce a madman" (p. 276). These are violent wanderers in a region of soul delimited on one side by the message on Wild Man's flak jacket—"Peace Through Fire Superiority"—and on the other by the answering one on Phony's—"Fuck It . . . Just Fuck It" (p. 104). Nobody goes home. With luck, somebody does what he has to do, and then just walks away. Somebody like Joker, for instance, who kills his friend the Cowboy, puts a terrible quick finish to the work of a sniper who has been blasting him away piece by methodical piece. Joker turns to what is left of the squad. Finally, he talks: "Man-oh-man," he says, "Cowboy looks like a bag of leftovers from a V.F.W. barbecue. Of course, I've got nothing

against dead people. Why, some of my best friends are dead"
(p. 153).

The scene, the talk, the irredeemably bleak emotional
tenor—all are exemplary. Although the product of strategies
ranging from the rather conventional "big" novel approach of
Better Times Than These to the compressed *cinéma vérité* of
The Short-Timers, the recent works of Vietnam fiction considered here do not include among their number a single one that
does not get down in one way or another to a similar vision of a
war operating at some absolute human bottom line. When it is
not pure insane atrocity, it is dismal black joke or, perhaps in
equal likelihood, some creepy unhinged combination of both.

In *Fields of Fire*, Baby Cakes and Ogre, a night away from
being taken prisoner and tortured to death (the discovery of
their mutilated bodies will lead in turn to the murder of two
Vietnamese), confer over a *Stars and Stripes* photograph of
American astronauts walking on the moon:

"Hey. Don't you want to see what it looks like?"
"I know what it looks like. It looks just like the Cu Bans."
Baby Cakes studied the picture again. "No. There ain't any trails."
[P. 219]

In *The Short-Timers*, Crazy Earl sits propped against a wall
during the battle for Hue. He leans over and lifts a hat brim
away from the face of the man sitting beside him holding a
beer. It is a dead enemy soldier. "Crazy Earl hugs the North
Vietnamese corporal," the narrator tells us. "He grins. 'I made
him sleep.' Crazy Earl puts his forefinger to his lips and whis-
pers, 'Shhh. He's resting now'" (p. 75).

In *Better Times Than These*, Operation "Western Movie" in
the Ia Drang finally supplies a young officer with the punch

line to a story he has heard once all the way back in the world from a pilot who has been to the valley before him. The story is about something called "The River Blindness." What is it? the lieutenant has asked intently. How does it come? The pilot leans across the table and answers with great drunken solemnity. "It's when you go down to the river," he says, "and get your *eyes* shot out" (p. 67).

Again and again in these novels, we come upon such versions of the ultimate Vietnam fable, the surreal inside joke that can somehow seem to mean nothing and everything all at once. They all suggest variations, finally, on what Michael Herr remembers hearing once from a Fourth Division Lurp, something he later realizes to be "as one-pointed and resonant," he says, "as any war story I ever heard, it took me a year to understand it: 'Patrol went up the mountain,'" the Lurp tells him. "'One man came back. He died before he could tell us what happened.' I waited for the rest," Herr goes on, "but it seemed not to be that kind of story; when I asked him what had happened he just looked like he felt sorry for me, fucked if he'd waste time telling stories to anyone dumb as I was" (p. 6).

A common quality of these novels is how they, too, often wind up a kind of spooky non-sequitur straining to extend itself into larger signification, some badass joke passing itself off as metaphysical fable. Yet connections do continue to get made in increasing measure, and, as with earlier Vietnam narrative, they come most frequently through the striking of new forms of alliance between experiential truth and a variety of distinctly literary modes of postulation. Groom's *Better Times Than These* and Webb's *Fields of Fire*, for instance, both attempts to write rather traditional "big" narratives of war, make explicit in many ways their sense of strong aesthetic affiliation. Groom dedicates his book to two old "soldiers," his father and

James Jones; Webb's young marine lieutenant is named Robert E. Lee Hodges. Both writers, like Jones, and Hemingway and Crane before him, find their great theme in relating the experience of war to the acquisition of some basic sense of moral manhood. Their structural strategies—the interweaving, for instance, of the novel's action with elements of social documentary, the microcosmic impulse that calls attention to the representativeness of the individual case—would also seem to place them in the line of Dos Passos, William March, and Norman Mailer.

Heinemann's, Durden's, and Hasford's novels, on the other hand, incline toward a vision more explicitly experimental, extend themselves more than occasionally into the domain of the "new" novel of war as written by Heller, Vonnegut, and Pynchon. The first, for example, while decidedly the most conventional of the three—indeed in more ways of a piece not with them but rather with *Better Times Than These* and *Fields of Fire*—nonetheless plays itself out in many moments of focal intensity in something like a reality warp, a dimension where the actual itself seems to have become at one with stoned chaotic imagining. In the "real" part of the book, Dosier, the protagonist, watches his buddy Quinn, wielding a captured AK-47 buttdown like an axe, reduce a Vietnamese corpse to a pinkish goo (pp. 262–63); he hears about "Fucken Rayburn, the dufus from Davenport," who has gone home and "fucked up his wife; catches her messing around with a couple Davenport cops; does her in with a butcher knife" (p. 103); on the pretense of an attempted escape, he himself blows the head off a captured VC ("I hated that gook alive," he remembers thinking, "and I hated his corpse") (p. 220). Apace, in Dosier's mind, there have come equally transfixing visions of fear and murder, children in a great house chanting "Die, die," and standing at the top rail of a long staircase and "tumbling the bodies out and over" and "General Westhisface . . . saying over and over 'They're damn fine killers, eh? Damn fine'" (pp. 160–61). Perception and nightmare have become wholly of a piece.

In Durden's Vietnam, "reality" is with even greater thoroughness mixed with the stuff of the mad grotesque. Deserters live in sybaritic reward. Privates guard a pig farm where villagers raise rice for animal feed in order to sell the animals and buy rice to eat themselves. Angelo Bruno Cocuzza, Crazy Dago, makes a killing on killing, gets rich on a numbers racket involving the prospective figure for South Vietnamese troops killed on any given day. "Alice in Wonderland was gettin' to be timid shit next to this," Hawkins confesses. It is a war that makes him realize at last that the man who wrote *Catch-22* probably "wasn't crazy enough" (p. 207).

In Hasford's *The Short-Timers*, bored marines spend their nights torching bunker rats, kissing them goodbye, biting off their charred tails and murmuring "Ummm . . . love them crispy critters" (p. 59). Rafter Man one-ups them all, makes ritual preparation for first combat by eating a wafer of flesh from a fellow marine, just disintegrated some few yards away and minutes earlier by a direct hit from a mortar. "It's crazy," says a machine gunner named Alice, a huge black who always walks point and collects VC feet that he carries in a shopping bag on his back. "It's just plain fucking crazy," he says. "I wish I was back in the world." Corporal Joker knows better. "No," he says, "back in the world is the crazy part. This, all this world of shit, this is real" (p. 104).

Corporal Joker knows better indeed. But he also knows that in any moment even the worst of what one has to take for real can somehow become its surreal other as well. Stopped outside

Hue city by a colonel who will eventually have him sent to the
field for failing to salute and for wearing a peace symbol, Joker
suddenly has a vision of the "poge" officer going to his jeep and
pulling "a poncho off a lump in the back seat. The lump is a
marine lance corporal in the fetal position. In the lance corporal's neck are punctures—many, many of them." Joker sees
himself looking back now at the face of his persecutor. "The
poge colonel grins," he says, "bares his vampire fangs, takes a
step toward me" (p. 117). Reality has gone all the way over to
the over side, connected up with its unreal obverse in one
awful seamless circuit. Hasford affirms the dictum from William Burroughs he has quoted earlier in a chapter epigraph: "A
psychotic is a guy who just found out what's going on" (p. 29).

The prize of experience for the Vietnam writer, as all these
novels again reveal, is the penetration of a strange midworld of
consciousness, a "country," once more to paraphrase Michael
Herr, that is "the war," a precinct of memory *and* imagining,
the two caught in some curious, perpetual suspension. Back in
what used to be the world at last, Philip Dosier writes nonetheless, "I have traveled to a place where the dead lie above the
ground in rows and bunches. Time has gone somewhere without me. This is not my country, not my time. I have not come
home, Ma. I have gone ahead, gone back" (p. 307). Corporal
Joker knows this as well, knows that "those of us who survive
to be short-timers will fly the great speckled bird back to
hometown America. But home won't be there anymore and we
won't be there either. Upon each of us the war has lodged itself,
a black crab feeding" (p. 151).

Recurrently this comes to stand as the lesson of sense-
making that most recent writers of the war hold in common,
an answer to that buzz and mutter of solitary consciousness,

that thing, to paraphrase Dosier, that hovers there "like a poltergeist, whispering" (p. 279). One must finally make a going back that is a going ahead as well.

It would seem almost as if in answer to this perception that among the newest novels of Vietnam there has finally come one more, Tim O'Brien's *Going after Cacciato*, a work not so much a synthesis of memory and imagination, life and art, as a testament to their utter fluid interchangeability. It is, thus, in effect, the form of its content. It is a book at once intensely "written," a conscious imaginative tour de force, and one that also somehow recaptures the truth of the experience as well in the whole impact of its concrete particularness and actuality. "Facts are one thing," a character in the novel muses at a certain point. "Interpretation," he goes on, "is something else" (p. 227). The task of the Vietnam writer, O'Brien seems to point out throughout the book, is to recognize the radicalness of this disparity yet in the same moment to realize that there may be a lens of consciousness, so to speak, through which it may be made to appear at least provisionally resolved. Somehow, the job will be "putting facts in the right framework" (p. 227), one in which the outlines of the two have become congruent and seemingly indistinguishable.

In more explicit terms, the process is also described by the character whose primary work it becomes, Specialist Fourth Class Paul Berlin: "Insight, vision. What you remember is determined by what you see, and what you see depends on what you remember. A cycle, Doc Peret had said. A cycle that has to be broken. And this requires a fierce concentration on the process itself: focus on the order of things, sort out the flow of events so as to understand how one thing led to another, search for that point at which what happened had been extended into a vision of what might have happened" (p. 207).

Yet as Doc Peret has also said, one always has to be careful about where one jumps in. If there is something called experience, something tangible that makes it possible for one to say, "This has happened, no mistake," there is also the possibility of a vacuum. If there is terror, pain, anger, there is also dead space, empty waiting for something that never comes. Consciousness can succumb to too much of that, go in and not come out. "No substance," he says, hence "no conceptual materiel" (p. 105). No substance equals no order. "Can't have order in vacuum. For order, you got to have substance, materiel. So here we are . . . nothing to order, no substance. Aimless, that's what it is: a bunch of kids trying to pin the tail on the Asian donkey. But no fuckin tail. No fuckin donkey" (p. 105).

One begins, then, takes at least a first step toward meaning, by not getting lost in the empty places, by concentrating on some definition of substance, "materiel." To use Berlin's own characterization of the problem, one gets to something like "the facts," reaches a point at which they are "not disputed." This he does, and even gets to the place where he can say, "Facts did not bother him. Billy Boy had died of fright. Buff was dead. Frenchie was dead. Pederson was dead. Sidney Martin and Bernie Lynn had died in tunnels. Those were all facts, and he could face them squarely" (p. 324). The fundamental fact of life, in sum, is the fact of death.

What does trouble one, Berlin admits, is "the order of facts—which facts came first and which came last, the relations among facts." There *is* still the problem "of keeping them straight" (pp. 324–25). Yet this, too, can be mastered, indeed must be mastered if one is eventually to proceed from memory, important enough in its own right, to new possibilities of meaning, so desperately needed, that can only be opened up by imagination. It is the cost of going ahead, Berlin discovers, that one must make a complete going back, a remembering of the totality of one's experience in all its hideous plenitude. So this too he does, assays it all from front to back, back to front, every nasty piece of it: Frenchie Tucker, shot through the nose, and Bernie Tucker with his tunnel wound; Billy Boy Watkins, dying of shock and fright, his foot blown off by a sputtering, seemingly harmless Bouncing Betty, screaming the way only the horribly wounded can scream and trying to lace back on the boot that holds what used to be his left leg from the shinbone down; Buff, ass-high in the air, tilted over like "a praying Arab in Mecca" (p. 283), his face, his eyes and nose and mouth and brains filling up to the muddy brim his upturned helmet.

Apace, the writer also finds himself well launched on the other half of the sense-making process, the necessary complement to the finding and the assembling in memory of "the facts," the search for "a way" as well "of tracing the possibilities" (pp. 172–73). To think on "what happened," as mentioned earlier, is to generate new reflection on "what might have happened" as its inevitable obverse. Now the novel's landscape of consciousness, so to speak, begins to complete itself, to fill out its larger configurations. As it defines its grand geography, its whole expanse of possible vision, it comes to encompass the ideas of both substance *and* structure, becomes a conflation of the worlds of experience and art alike. It is at once a terrain on which are played out Paul Berlin's actual memories of the war as he stands guard during a single night on the coast of Quang Ngai Province and the ground as well of his visionary postulation of a search for one Cacciato, the archetypal platoon idiot, after he has made a personal farewell to arms, walked away from the war on the start of an odyssey that ultimately takes him and his band of GI pursuers from the Laotian border to Delhi, Teheran, Kabul, Athens, across the Balkans, through

Zagreb, Graz, Berlin, Bonn, all the way along the winding dusty road to Paris.

Cacciato, "dumb as a bullet," Stink Harris has called him. "Dumb as a month-old oyster fart," Harold Murphy has muttered (p. 2). Cacciato, the basic-issue grunt, dumb enough to go fishing in "the world's greatest lake country" in bomb-crater ponds floating with the bodies of dead NVA (pp. 238–42). Cacciato, a vision of one simple spirit, dumb and dogged and maybe just indomitable enough to think he can take a long walk out alive, get to Paris, find peace.

Then there are his pursuers. The war follows him in microcosm. There is Berlin, the memory-dreamer; Doc Peret, the philosopher-skeptic and all-purpose savant; Sarkin Aung Wan, the Indochinese girl who knows from the start that "the way in . . . is the way out," that "to go home one must become a refugee" (p. 89); Corson, the old, broken lieutenant, who knows that it has not been his war ever, that it has been something without "heart," just an ugly mess in which "nobody likes nobody" (p. 150); Oscar Johnson, badass Detroit black, apostle of the realities, who knows that nothing is over until the GI patrol does what it has to, catches "the dude" and drops him "on the bargaining table" (p. 313); Eddie Lazutti, "who loved to sing" (p. 141); and Stink Harris, "daring when the odds looked good" (p. 143), mean, narrow, alternately fawning and cruel, yet finally loyal even unto death.

On a landscape of consciousness so broadly set out, and through this array of characters that Herman Melville would have described as an "Anacharsis Clootz deputation of mankind,"[9] a kind of grand compendium of every species of "war story" one might conceive of goes about the process of getting itself told. Some of the stories seem mainly a product of brute remembered fact, others the stuff of surreal imagining, still others the result of some curious combination of both. Some start out literally true only to get made truer than true through strange transformations worked by the processes of art.

Many "war stories," Berlin warns us, sounding a good deal like Michael Herr on hearing the "real" story of the platoon that went up the mountain, are "hackneyed and unprofound," obvious elemental truths looking for a final line that would somehow make them seem more striking or significant "It hurts to be shot," he writes. "Dead men are heavy. Don't seek trouble, it'll find you soon enough. You hear the shot that gets you. Scared to death on the field of battle. Life after death. These were hard lessons, true, but they were the lessons of ignorance; ignorant men, trite truths."[10] The only thing that "remained" a good deal of the time, he goes on, "was the simple event. The facts, the physical things. A war like any war. No new messages. Stories that began and ended without transition. No developing drama or tension or direction. No order" (pp. 288–89).

A lesson, a message, a truth, in sum, could come off as so simple that it seemed a kind of Orphic movement to the very fulcrum of reality. The simpler better. "Don' ever get shot," Oscar Johnson tells Eddie Lazutti:

> "There it is," said Eddie Lazutti.
> "Never. Don' never get shot."
> "Tell it man."
> "I told it. Never." [P. 287]

Yet the same simple lessons of the war, banal, unprofound, stupid as at times they seemed to be, could also for all their simplicity turn maddeningly complex. These were the lessons often of "The Things They Didn't Know" (p. 262). These were simple truths that too frequently got bigger and uglier and more perplexing than anyone could handle. They fought the war where they did, suffered and died, made Quang Ngai suffer and die with them, for "the luck of the draw, bad fortune, forces beyond reckoning" (p. 265). They fought, most of them, for "no beliefs" (p. 272), just "survival" (p. 265). "They fought the war but no one took sides" (p. 272). "They did not know good from evil" (p. 273).

All this we learn as Paul Berlin in a single moment stands on his observation post by the South China Sea *and* makes his way after Cacciato on the road to Paris, combines experiential memory with imaginative invention, brings the truth of what was and the truth of what might have been into strange illuminating congruency. Small meanings arising from the experience become large meanings and vice versa. Fact mixes with fantasy, the brute actual with outright surreal illusion. Billy Boy Watkins does indeed die "of fright," does die truly "scared to death," the narrator tells us, "on the field of battle" (p. 1). Others, if they in their fates do not make ever for so nearly interesting a figure, suggest "stories" at least as striking in their power to appall, if for no other reason precisely because of their bleak matter-of-factness. Here truly is literature as literal body count, and vice versa. Frenchie Tucker and Bernie Lynn and Pederson and Ruby Chassler and Buff and Ready Mix have one by one entered their names on the swelling roster of the dead. Lieutenant Sidney Martin has gotten fragged. Vaught has shaved down his white, rain-dead skin with a bayonet, caught a fungus, and wound up in a hospital in Japan without an arm.

Apace, the work leaps from this sense of the utter unreality of the real often to its pure obverse. On the stage of consciousness created here, there is room for the playing out in life of figurative cliché, popular myth, even geopolitical shibboleth.

Invoking the shades of Bing Crosby, Bob Hope, and Dorothy Lamour, for instance, cinematic ghosts from an earlier, better war, and mocking at the same time the public-relations hyperbole once exploited by Kissinger and Nixon in the name of what quickly became the charade of a negotiated peace, the pursuers of Cacciato move along "The Road to Paris." They fall through a hole in the road, land in the ultimate VC tunnel, a kind of final, meta-underground, learn from their intelligent and remarkably sympathetic adversary that there is no light at the end of it or any other tunnel for anyone, that they are all, echoing Hasford's observation, "prisoners" of the same war. This is a war indeed that looks rather uniform in its ugly senselessness, they later find, from both ends of the periscope. It is mainly a matter of perspective.

Later, imprisoned in Iran by the Shah's dreaded SAVAK, they find that this is also pretty much the case with something called Geneva Accords. It all depends on how one reads them. By now it is no matter, though. Their government, they are told, "does not know" them. "Or chooses not to" (p. 230). To get out of this one and go on, they will have to make their own way.

This they do, even to the end. Finally, as morning breaks in the observation post, and Berlin recalls "how on his very first day he had witnessed the ultimate war story" (p. 208), about a boy who got "SCARED TO DEATH IN THE REPUBLIC OF VIETNAM" (p. 217), the novel also reaches the end of the road to Paris. As Berlin finally goes back in experiential memory to where all the death began, so in the realm of invention the voice of Sarkin Aung Wan calls to him also across a Paris negotiating table to go forward into new life as well. "The refugee must do more than flee," she tells him. "He must arrive. He must return at last to a world as it is, however much in conflict with his hopes, and he must then do what he can to edge reality toward what he has dreamed, to change what he can change, to go beyond the wish or the fantasy" (p. 320).

Yet Berlin has a point to make across the table too. Attractive as Sarkin Aung Wan's appeal may sound, "even in imagination," Berlin says, "we must obey the logic of what we started. Even in imagination we must be true to our obligations, for, even in imagination, obligation cannot be outrun. Imagination, like reality, has its limits" (p. 323). This is all to say that if imagination can in fact dictate the character of future experience, it must also be seen in many ways as having its own character dictated by the memory of experience past.

The negotiations are at an impasse. As the novel ends, Berlin is in Vietnam, back in the legion of the "fuckups. Dipsticks in the overall slime" (p. 329). Trying to extend a vision of what happened into a vision of what might have happened has been simply an exercise of consciousness in the middest, a testing out of the limits of sense-making. It has been at best a showing of the way. One imagines only in terms of the pull of memory; one comes to terms with memory only through the pull of imagining. Here is the strange mid-world where progress toward perhaps the truest telling of all has at most just begun to be made.[11]

A similar vision of the middest, as I have noted earlier, has also from the outset been characteristic of the Vietnam dramas of David Rabe. In *The Basic Training of Pavlo Hummel* and *Sticks and Bones*, the domain of the creative artifact has served as an autonomous, "open" precinct of vision where it has been possible at once both to suggest a sense of the awesome, harrowing reality of Vietnam as experience and also to address that reality in terms of something like collective mythic consciousness as well. So with *Streamers*, a play effectively completing a trilogy. Precisely to the degree, in fact, that it enacts the visionary design of *Going after Cacciato* essentially in mirror image—the country that is the war extended backward, so to speak, to incorporate the stateside barracks room, a vision of what may happen becoming in effect the determinant of much that actually does happen—it reveals the unique serviceability of that design as a centralizing mode of literary response. To put this in more familiar terms, just as the self-consciously literary and even "mythic" quality of *Streamers* seems predicated on some strange interplay between memory and imagination in an essentially aesthetic sense, so it is precisely by being about that interplay that the drama also achieves its intense air of human actuality.

Indeed, if *Streamers*, is "about" anything, it is about the effects of a "memory" of something called Vietnam upon a group of soldiers mainly who have never been there, who have to conceive of its threat as almost pure imaginative projection, and who in turn allow imaginative projection to turn itself most deadly real in bitter experiential fact. Conversely, the bearer of this "memory," the one character in the play who has already been out there, is an aging, boozy, career NCO, lost almost completely in his own world of make-believe, of dreams of better wars, of the camaraderie of the airborne, of heroism in Korea, of anything but what his most recent war just was.

The war is there, then, in *Streamers*, as some weird amalgam of memory and imagining, at once a curse and a terrible prophecy. The Army that died a good deal of the time in Vietnam of its own self-torturing misery, its enlistment in the service of random, multiform violence to no discernible end, finds itself imaged in microcosm and contained in a single squad bay about to explode of its own awful inside tension. Macho posturing jangles with homoerotic threat and insinuation. Lifer and draftee, officer and enlisted man, black and white, hold together in a tense, fragile symbiosis only a soul's breath away from horror.

The horror comes in the person of Carlyle, a hard, sullen, violent black draftee. Strutting his mean, ugly anger, he brings out the dark latencies that in each of the play's other characters have for the moment been lying barely submerged. He confronts Roger, another black, whose closest friend has been a white soldier named Billy, with the easy fiction of his hunger for white acceptance, and taunts him with the prospect of his fate as a black man in a white man's army. With an overt homosexual come-on, he exploits the fears and miseries of the edgy, epicene Richie, who has previously divided most of his time between emotional backbiting and worrying about being "queer." This grotesque, almost demonic preying of Carlyle's on Richie in turn draws out the violence hiding in Billy, an average, decent, even thoughtful boy. Suddenly he finds himself confronting Carlyle with a razor and screaming, "THIS IS RIDICULOUS. I NEVER FACED ANYBODY IN MY LIFE WITH ANYTHING TO KILL THEM. YOU UNDERSTAND ME? I DON'T HAVE A GODDAMN THING ON THE LINE HERE!" (pp. 87–88).

It is too late. The thing on the line, for no particular reason, is his life. He dies, stabbed and sliced to a huddled, whimpering lump by Carlyle's switchblade. This is the fate also of the old NCO Rooney, running into the room from a drunken game of hide-and-seek with his buddy Cokes, just home from the war. Rooney has just received his orders for Vietnam. Effectively, he has died there just as surely as if he had gone.

The melting-pot, macho army, the repository of old marching songs, of patriotic slogans, of a whole accumulated legacy of warrior myth, hemorrhages to death in a frenzy of internal convulsion. What is left at the end of *Streamers*—after the

MPs have come and gone with their predictably officious lieutenant—is a tired old drunken NCO ("they" say he has leuke-
mia, but he thinks he keeps falling down just because he drinks
so much) home from a war he cannot even understand enough
to talk about, and a couple of scared privates, one black, of dubious racial identity, and the other white, of equally dubious
sexuality. They are the remaining specimens of American
manhood.

In the old sergeant's head, there comes back the melody of an
old airborne song, the tune and a few cocky lines that tell how
a paratrooper can look at death and laugh:

> Beautiful Streamer
> Open for me,
> The sky is above me,
> But no canopy

Words begin to come out with the melody, but they are not English. Rather, they come "in a makeshift language imitating
Korean," and the song slowly becomes "a dream, a lullaby, a
farewell, a lament" (p. 109). He sings, as the lights go out, a
song for the last war, not knowing even now that the next one
has already done its terrible work.

Bringing the war home through the combined activities of
memory and imagination is similarly the strategy at the heart
of the most recent book of poems constituting a major and significant response to Vietnam, Bruce Weigl's *A Romance*. Whatever the war once was or might have been, it is now as much
explicitly "here" as "there," well along in the process of being
assimilated out of essentially private consciousness and into
some larger context of collective myth. Predictably, on just

these grounds, *A Romance* is not nearly so spectacular or apocalyptic a book as John Balaban's *After Our War*, nor does it dwell with such obsessive concern on visions of the conflict itself as do earlier works such as D. C. Berry's *Saigon Cemetery*, Michael Casey's *Obscenities*, or the two major veterans' anthologies, *Winning Hearts and Minds* and the more recent *Demilitarized Zones*. It is, rather, albeit in a somewhat muted, domestic variation, a genuine attempt to emulate the values of the literary type imaged in its title: it is truly a quest, a movement of consciousness through and even beyond experience toward some large and possibly redeeming imaginative wisdom. It is also, to be sure, an intentional mock-type, a romance for unheroic and perhaps even antiheroic times. Yet it also seeks, as traditional romance and epic have always done, to accommodate cultural memory within some larger structure of collective myth, to be both a ritualized formal remembrance of the times and a liberation from them toward some final vision of other times and better.

This would seem to be the point of opening the book with a poem concocted from a hodgepodge of conventional romance paraphernalia so outlandish in their contemporary reconstitution as to create a sense of their own novel, almost surreal authority. There is the dream vision, the wounded warrior arising from his infirmity, the voyage, the new epic quest, the siren call of the faraway remembered land, the place half sinister hallucination and half magical fantasy. "In my dream of the hydroplane," the poet begins, "I'm sailing toward Bien Hoa / the shrapnel in my thighs / like tiny glaciers." He continues:

> I remember a flower,
> a kit, a mannikin playing the guitar,

> a yellow fish eating a bird, a truck
> floating in urine, a rat carrying a banjo,
> a fool counting the cards, a monkey praying,
> a procession of whales, and far off
> two children eating rice,
> speaking French—
> I'm sure of the children,
> their damp flutes
> the long line of their vowels.

Here is a quest for our times. Like much of the recent literature of the war, it is both a going back and a going beyond. Grotesquerie and sordor and foolishness mix with visions of elemental wonder and even beauty. The imagination of romance, in a world of remembered madness, the poet seems to say, can still launch us in consciousness toward new understandings of the eternal and real that have perhaps been there from the start. "I'm sure of the children," he concludes, "their damp flutes / the long line of their vowels." Out of the dream of wounds and chaos there emerges the rich, still sound of the music of life.

A similar quality and movement of consciousness characterize the work's title poem. It might be best described as a treatise on modern chivalry, the somewhat less than noble art of contemporary American quixotism. In a bar, his "lust like a flag," the narrator ogles "a skinny red-haired girl" wearing

> beneath the white points of her pelvis
> an enormous belt buckle
> shaped like the head of a snake
> with two red rhinestone eyes

> which she polishes with the heels of her hands
> making circles on her own fine things.

She is Eve and Circe and the eternal honky-tonk woman, and the narrator is the chevalier weighing out his old ideas of martial and amatory feats:

> It is always like this with me in bars,
> wanting women I know
> I'll have to get my face
> punched bloody to love.

It is always like this, he tells us, with the warrior virtues, to fight, to conquer, and maybe later on to tell tales of prowess:

> I don't sleep anyway so I go to bars
> and tell my giant lies to women
> who have heard them from me,
> from the thousands of me
> out on the town with our impossible strategies
> for no good reason but ourselves
> who are holy.

In every romance in every bar, there he is, the American, the thwarted hero, plying his "impossible strategies," too far gone in his self-mocking parody of romantic aspiration to remember how it might have ever been worth his pains.

Unlike "Sailing to Bien Hoa," "A Romance" seems to have no explicit connection with the experience of Vietnam in particular. Yet in its parody of a warrior ideal, the narrator's drunken, futile obsession with one last brawl or one better lie that will affirm some lingering notion of his own sanctity, his debased romance of a search after some grotesque, half-forgotten idea of heroism, it tells us rather precisely about a condition of spirit that seems in many ways to have gotten us to Vietnam in the first place and in retrospect likewise seems at least one thing that makes the burden of it so hard to cast off. Why does this narrator not sleep at night? What are his giant falsehoods about? We cannot be sure that Vietnam especially has anything to do with all this. Yet that in a way would seem to be Weigl's point. Americans are walking war stories.

In corresponding ways, so nearly all the poems explicitly about Vietnam in the volume most generally point away from a vision of the war itself toward matters of common apprehension. Most of them exist in a dimension of consciousness where memory has become so interfused with broad-ranging attributes of imaginative invention that they are justly no longer the property of the veteran or the survivor alone, but of us all. So it is, for instance, with "Monkey." "My monkey from Vietnam," the narrator calls it, "My monkey." "It makes no sense," he confesses a few lines later:

> I beat the monkey.
> I didn't know him.
> He was bloody.
> He lowered his intestines
> to my shoes. My shoes
> spit-shined the moment
> I learned to tie the bow.

Senseless as it may seem, he tells us, what American boys found to kill in Vietnam was waiting for them from the day that learning to tie shoes was allowed to get inevitably connected up with the idea of a GI spit shine and vice versa. Yet one can only try to live with that now, he goes on to tell us in the next stanza, try to live with it honestly, sadly. "I'm twenty-five years old, / quiet, tired of the same mistakes," he says, "the same greed, the same past." One must above all be patient:

> If we're soldiers we should smoke them
> if we have them. Someone's bound
> to point us in the right direction
> sooner or later.

Still, the enterprise need not be carried out alone. "I'm tired," he admits at a certain point, "and I'm glad you asked." To be sure, he says at the same time, the basic story has not gotten any saner or better:

> There is a hill.
> Men run to top hill.
> Men take hill.
> Give hill to man.

But there are at least now others to help with the task, carry on the movement of consciousness toward sense-making:

> Me and my monkey
> and me and my monkey
> my Vietnamese monkey
> my little brown monkey
> came with me
> to Guam and Hawaii
> in Ohio he saw
> my people he

> jumped on my daddy
> he slipped into mother
> he baptized my sister
> he's my little brown monkey
> he came here from heaven
> to give me his spirit imagine
> my monkey my beautiful
> monkey he saved me lifted
> me above the punji
> sticks above the mines
> above the ground burning
> above the dead above
> the living above the
> wounded dying the wounded
> dying

We carry the monkey. The monkey carries us. By the end it is back to the old business. The old pointless reality does not seem much changed from what it was earlier:

> Men take hill away from smaller men.
> Men take hill and give to fatter man.
> Men take hill. Hill has number.
> Men run up hill. Run down.

Memory nags; it will not give up. If there has been a moment of imaginative self-transcendence, a collective sharing of the burden, it has been brief. Still, it is again far more than we had before the endeavor of sense-making began.

It is the poet's task, Weigl seems to demonstrate again and again, to search for those moments when consciousness can arrive at some point of strange, creative equidistance between memory and imagination, moments of spiritual epiphany in which the return through memory to experience can become at the same time an access to the imaginative means of liberation from its terrible omnipresence.

This would seem to be the point in both formal and thematic terms, for instance, of "Him, on the Bicycle." It is a poem that begins deep in memory, in a too-familiar incident of war: above, a helicopter, door gun ablaze; below, "four men running carrying rifles," and "one man on a bicycle." The critical moment comes; just as the tracers seem about to strike home, the man and the dream of remembered death drag the narrator out of the air and into their domain:

> He pulls me out of the ship,
> there's firing far away.
> I'm on the back of the bike
> holding his hips.
> It's hard pumping for two,
> I hop off and push the bike.

Yet precisely as he becomes most fully possessed by the earth below and its vision of mortal terror, he also begins movement as well toward that other, better point of vision at which he becomes imaginatively released:

> I'm brushing past trees,
> the man on the bike stops pumping
> lifts his feet,
> we don't waste a stroke.
> His hat flies off,
> I catch it behind my back,
> put it on, I want to live forever!

> Like a blaze
> streaming down the trail.

The man on the bicycle in experiential and visionary terms
alike is both our burden and our redemption. In some new dimension of consciousness where memory and imagining can at
last be reconciled, he calls us to a breakneck, thrilling race, an
ecstasy of flight toward a vision of our common humanity.

For the most part, however, the romance of consciousness,
the poet tells us, will be far less ecstatic. Mostly it will just be
living with Vietnam like a bad dream that only gets better
when we rise to some small eminence of vision that makes it
seem so at least for the moment. Sometimes we can put its
darkness to rout with the light of imaginative wish:

> one day I'm back in the army
> a nameless private in a crack
> platoon. We never see the enemy
> Yet we have wonderful statistics.
>
> Next day a crippled friend
> walks across the room,
> tells me his paralysis was unreal,
> thin steel sliver.

Our more usual means of illumination, however, will come in
the mid-range at best, and, more likely if anywhere, back a
good deal toward the old memory:

> Occasionally in this zone
> I'm handed a mirror.

I look at my face,
find it gaunt but interesting,

my eyes are innocent
without passion or desire
my smile slightly twisted.

There is where the effort will have to be made: crooked smile
and all, keeping on; accepting the fact that the face is gaunt and
given over to a kind of empty stare, but still trying to find out
what makes it interesting; staying with the business of making
sense. For Weigl, for all the writers of Vietnam, that will remain the object, the last heroism.

6.

Conclusion

It was just the scrawniest goddamn defense. All we had was hand-held weapons, nothing. I got Spooky on line to help us out. Spooky is a C-47 airplane with Gatling guns. I got him up and, oh, it was nice to hear because we started making contact and had some pretty heavy automatics against us. I remember in the middle of the night when I really thought we were all going to get eaten, Spooky came up and called me, saying, "Hello, hello, this is Spooky zero-two with forty thousand rounds of happiness." And, oh, happy to see him. . . .

To see your friends killed, hear about them being killed, it was . . . A little piece of you gets killed each time.

Al Santoli, *Everything We Had*

We had one officer—a good one—who just leaped up in the middle of a fire fight and said, "It's just kids and they're all fucking dying. Just kids, kids, kids." They had to take him away.

Use kids to fight a war—if you're going to use anybody. They're the best. They're still learning. They can hump the hills. They can take it. And they don't take it personal. . . .

You get an attitude: They can kill you, but they can't eat you. Don't sweat the small stuff. My men used to say, "There it is. There it fucking is, Lieutenant." Like, what are you going to tell me, what are you going to show me? What is it in the scheme of things that is going to give me any more insight on the whole situation? You ain't showing me shit. Dead is dead. That's it.

Mark Baker, *Nam*

t is somehow appropriate that the title of the last chapter of a book on Vietnam and the problem of sense-making should claim to deliver by symbolic pronouncement what the book itself is hardly in a position to yield up in fact. One proceeds with great care on the subject of conclusions about a body of literature characterized perhaps most visibly of all by continuing growth and change. One can only attempt a kind of summary evaluation and some speculative comment about possible directions for the future.

These things can be done with at least reasonable confidence, I believe, because of the emergence in Vietnam writing of what I have earlier described as a certain identifiable centrality of vision, an understanding that just as the "real" war itself so often proved a hopeless tangle of experiential fact and projected common myth, so a "true" literary comprehending of it would come only as a function of experiential remembrance *and* imaginative invention considered in some relationship of near-absolute reflexiveness. It would have to come of some new architecture of consciousness founded—and often in the most radical terms of juxtaposition and even reversal—on an awareness of the degree to which each had ultimately to be seen as implying and indeed quite probably entailing the sense-making possibilities of the other.

Somewhere along the line, everyone seems to have realized, like Michael Herr's ocean-eyed lurp, that any attempt to tell just the "story" of Vietnam alone would always wind up a fable without a last line, some unwittingly crafted exercise in chilling existential non sequitur. And at approximately the same point, nearly everyone seems to have realized also that trying to write *Catch-22* about *Catch-22* would come off mainly as pure manic transcription with a last line seemingly thrown down where none was needed, a case of aesthetic invention casting itself into strained parodic after-image of a thing in its reality altogether beyond invention from the start.

To address this point more directly, one might consider, for instance, several recent additions to the body of Vietnam writing, all published after I had completed the foregoing portions of this text. One is a novel, Charles Coleman's *Sergeant Back Again*,[1] a challenging, intelligent, painful book about the war-haunted inmates of a psycho ward in a Stateside army medical center, and about their attempts, some successful and some monstrously failed, to put off the madness of the war that has in one way or another seized them to the farthest depths of being. Two others, *Everything We Had* by Al Santoli and *Nam* by Mark Baker,[2] come under the relatively new heading of oral history, the first a series of extended reflections by thirty-three veterans, of suggestively diverse background and involvement, and the second a complex ordering of anonymous comment, through strategies resembling most closely those of cinematic montage, into a narrative devised thematically to recapitulate in a most general and comprehensive sense the unfolding of one's vision of the experience as a whole, before, during, and after.

In light of what has been said earlier in my own comments about the radical eclecticism of mode and intention that so often endows Vietnam writing, particularly that of recent years, with its quality of distinctly "creative" truth-telling, the reviews of the works described, one a consciously literary fiction and the others at least presumably oriented in the direction of something like fact, make for suggestive reading indeed. With regard to *Sergeant Back Again*, more than one writer commented on the sense of profound experiential authority that pervaded the narrative, seemed in fact its most compelling feature. Evident throughout was the author's deep commitment to telling a story that was clearly his own and that of the men he himself had come to know and care for most deeply ten years earlier. Accordingly, a common view as a result was that the attempt to devise various fictive modes of representation—"official" documentary reports, dramatized renditions of counseling interviews and experiments in group therapy, reconstructions of free-flowing dream-fantasy and harrowed psycho-nightmare—came close to being an unneeded embellishment upon materials that might perhaps have been even more powerfully dealt with had they been left as unmediated case history.[3]

By way of interesting reversal, discussions of both the oral documentaries centered often not so much on their frequently acute rendering of experience in all its complex actuality as on what struck reviewers almost paradoxically as the uncanny literariness of the various passages in which this effect of utter intense veracity seemed to be most fully achieved. If they seemed noteworthy for their projection of a sense, as one writer observed, of the decisively truth-burdened immediacy one associates with the most accomplished examples of experiential witness, they also seemed to suggest at the same time an equally important quality of sense-making achievement in their recurrent, almost startlingly routine demonstration of clearly "aesthetic" attributes of focus and design, point, coherence, and closure.[4]

There it is. Self-consciously imaginative art that compels us to attend more than in any way else to what seems the almost unbearable intensity of its experiential resonance. And the witness of personal memory that repeatedly calls attention to what seems its strange, unsettling literariness. There, in the terms of art at least, is the country that remains the war, a precinct of consciousness somewhere between memory and imagination, a realm where each seems empowered to signify to greatest effect precisely in those moments when it becomes informed most fully by the other.

"The point of this is that we, gentlemen, we *have* to make some sense of this. We have to make some sense of ourselves." So, in *Sergeant Back Again*, speaks Pollard, the mad, broken, scholar-intelligence specialist, who now attempts to engineer a pact among his fellow psychic victims to get to "the truth of what happened, and why it happened" (p. 64), at whatever the cost, even if in the process the chance of thereby coming back instead eclipses itself into the final certainty of no return. For Pollard himself, the latter likelihood proves the case. But there is also the young surgical specialist named Collins, the one soldier who does come through by going all the way back, abandoning himself to flight and darkness, casting himself down in the muck of a Texas riverbed and spending a last solitary terrible night in frenzied reenactment of what he has undergone, forming in clay effigy a "yearbook," his young psychiatrist Captain Nieland tells him, a "catalogue," a "sum total" of all the dead Americans he once tried so desperately to keep alive. Collins returns from this to realize that "the possibility of making some sense of the non sense was not the futile plea of a madman" (p. 236). As the novel concludes, he is, appropriately, now the author, just beginning to write it, the story about "himself and Pollard and Captain Nieland" (p. 237). The fiction of experience in turn becomes the basis of new fictive inquiry, ongoing sense-making design.

In the foreword to *Sergeant Back Again*, the author is at pains to describe himself as "mainly a chronicler who was left no choice but to try to speak for the inarticulate, the psychically scarred, and the wasted." It is not his book, he avers, even after the long transit from experience to ordered aesthetic expression, but still the war's. "I did not make this story," he writes; "it came that way, ready-made, defined by historical circumstances, generated by the soldiers who have had to fight the most insidious and intimate battle: the one with yourself."

Now, in the solitude of consciousness, as once amidst the hubbub and jostle of grim actuality, an idea of fictive order for the war calls attention more than in any way else to its strange congruity with the design of fact. And so apace, in the narratives of Santoli and Baker, as if through bizarre mirror image, fact likewise seems to make its most visible meanings by recurrently calling attention in more than any way else to its inherent and essential fictiveness.

Here are four brief illustrations on the point:

I was a grunt radioman. So I used to hang back with the CO and keep squads together. I got to watch the whole war with my eyes. I loved to just sit in the ditch and watch people die. As bad as that sounds, I just liked to *watch* no matter what happened, sitting back with my homemade cup of hot chocolate. It was like a big movie. [*Nam*, p. 93]

We found out later that day that it was a division that our company was butting up against. But all we ever saw were a couple of sneaker marks and a couple of sweat shirts with UCLA on them. We started wondering who in the hell we were fighting. We're wet and freezing in the monsoon, and these NVA dudes got UCLA sweat shirts. [*Nam*, p. 168]

Anyway, me and Don made five or six trips over there. Finally ended up setting up a .50-caliber. We couldn't get it working right, and we had been fighting for so goddamn long, got so irritated, ended up in a god-

Conclusion

damn fistfight. Man, we were surrounded by these motherfuckers and me and Don were fighting over who was going to get to shoot the .50. [*Everything We Had*, p. 85]

A lot of times we would sit in a bush as close as two or three feet from a trail and watch people walk back and forth for hours until somebody came along with a gun, and then we'd grab them, just reach right out of the bush and grab them by the ankles. This is like you're walking by a bush that you've seen every day in your life, and all of a sudden there's somebody in that bush that reaches out and grabs you. [*Everything We Had*, pp. 210–11]

One can open up Baker's and Santoli's books and find passages such as the ones quoted almost at random. In them one comes face to face with an intense, almost ruthless quality of experiential truth-telling and at the same time with a sense of craft or design so final, so utterly nailed down in its seeming completeness and inevitability as to be somehow beyond anything that conscious craft or design could of themselves have produced. On a routine patrol in a routine afternoon of the war, a contact mission turns into the usual murder: "I look around and everything is on fire, bathed in red. I can see tracers going out, tracers coming in. People are yelling and screaming. Pop, pop, pop, small arms fire. Fast pops, automatic weapons fire. Total chaos." Not chaos enough, though; not enough to get on without its own peculiar bit of crowning insanity. "Above it all," the narrator tells us by way of conclusion, "somebody had left a radio on in a hootch and it was Mary Hopkins singing that song, 'Goodbye'" (*Nam*, p. 64). Meanwhile, on another day in another place, one more mine spends itself upward into matter-of-fact, predictable mayhem: "*Boom*! Just like that and a guy is missing a leg, somebody is missing a foot. Everything stops for a second and there's a lot of action on the radio. A chopper comes down to pick him up. *Zoom*, he's gone." Apace, this time in consciousness, the horror again finds its sudden echo, some strange music of the unreal casting into absolute fixity of perception that which has at once become almost too immediate and real to be borne. "Boy," the narrator remembers thinking, "there's going to be a lot of people walking around after this war with no feet" (*Nam*, p. 100).

Repeatedly, it is there: the line, the idea, the image, the eerie epiphany that brings one more piece of the vision into absolute relief once and for all. It arises again out of the strange clamor and roar of the actual or gets summoned back from an old, barely remembered dream of intuition. It is the memory of the real war seeking out its point of interfusion with the unreal other that must so often, it would seem again and again, complete the pattern of its ultimate signification.

One senses in increasing measure that not only here, but across the whole spectrum of literary activity, this is something like a "natural" development. The story does truly seem to be well on toward finding its context. I am not suggesting, to be sure, that this therefore makes it inevitable that some grand literary synthesis of memory and invention will in this year or the next tell us at last everything we need to know about the experience of Vietnam once and for all. To demonstrate the folly of predictions such as that, one need only point to the recent example of William Manchester's *Good-Bye Darkness*,[5] a memoir of the 1941–45 war in the Pacific written fully thirty-five years after the event—a book of immense experiential authority and yet also, in terms of the triumph of imaginative apprehension it represents as well, a creative achievement of such original and almost terrifying beauty that one simply senses it could not have been written a moment sooner than it was.

Conclusion

There are still no books quite like that about the experience of Vietnam. There is no sense of commanding perspective, of some great and awful burden of remembrance imaginatively mastered and brought into the province of collective understanding in a way that might let it be put behind once and for all. A representative valedictory for Vietnam at this point would probably have to read more along the lines of the witness offered in *Everything We Had* by a black GI—appropriately, a spokesman in many ways for those Americans who often suffered in the war perhaps as much as any of their countrymen possibly could have, and who are still most painfully finding their way back:

I knew this guy. I could remember how many times a day he pissed, that's how well I knew the guy. We was really close, man, close. He was a Sicilian and I always used to kid him: "Hey you think I could join the family when we get out of here?" This guy was so close that he should have been my brother, but . . . he died. [P. 156]

He died. The black GI goes on. "I just can't," he says, ". . . sometimes, man . . . every time I talk about it, it just hurts." The black GI is right. It just hurts. As he once paid the price of going to the country that was the war, he now pays, through the effort of sense-making, the price of coming back. For him, for all the writers represented here, for all of us who care to read what they have to say, the war is not over. It will only be over when we have made it so through a common effort of signification, when we have learned at what cost it was waged for everyone it touched then and now and beyond. Then it will be over. Then we can say good-bye to it. Not before.

Notes

Preface

1. Paul Fussell, *The Great War and Modern Memory* (New York: Oxford University Press, 1975), p. ix.
2. Henry James, "The Art of Fiction," in *The Portable Henry James* (New York: Viking Press, 1968), p. 399.

I. Situation Report: The Experience of Vietnam

1. Michael Herr, *Dispatches* (New York: Alfred A. Knopf, 1977), pp. 9, 11.
2. Ronald J. Glasser, *365 Days* (New York: George Braziller, 1971), p. 109.
3. David Halberstam, *One Very Hot Day* (New York: Houghton Mifflin, 1967), p. 127.
4. Charles Durden, *No Bugles, No Drums* (New York: Viking Press, 1976), p. 11.
5. There has been an inclination, in recent films especially, to dream up ideas of breathtaking anomaly such as this— the surfing scenes, for instance, in *Apocalypse Now*, or the recurrent metaphor, in *The Deer Hunter*, of Russian roulette. Often it has led to symbolic overkill, Vietnam as aesthetico-philosophical conceit, when anyone who cared

to look could find as much of the surreal incongruous as might be wished in the thing itself.

6. Norman Mailer, "Mailer's Reply," response to a statement of opposition to the war by the editors of the *Paris Review*, reprinted in *Cannibals and Christians* (New York: Dial Press, 1966), p. 85.

7. I have never found any verification for this. When I was in Vietnam in 1969–70, however, it was still going around. In Patton's old command, the Eleventh Armored Cavalry, I heard it repeated so many times that it finally did not matter whether it happened or not. The story had acquired a reality of its own.

8. The officer was Brigadier General Mike Healy. See James Jones, *Viet Journal* (New York: Delacorte Press, 1973), p. 79.

9. Philip Caputo, *A Rumor of War* (New York: Holt, Rinehart & Winston, 1977), p. 4.

10. Gustav Hasford, *The Short-Timers* (New York: Harper & Row, 1979), p. 137.

2. American Literature: Prophecy and Context

1. Herman Melville, *Moby-Dick* (New York: Bobbs-Merrill, 1964), pp. 303, 30, 82.

2. To be more specific, the term, as Michael Herr observes, that translated most clearly in Vietnam to the expression for *jungle* in the language of its native tribes—"what its people," he says, "had always called it" (*Dispatches*, p. 10).

3. Ward Just, *Military Men* (New York: Alfred A. Knopf, 1970), p. 6.

4. Larry Heinemann, *Close Quarters* (New York: Farrar, Straus & Giroux, 1977), pp. 262–63.
5. Tim O'Brien, *Going after Cacciato* (New York: Delacorte Press/Seymour Lawrence, 1978), pp. 68–70, 283–87.
6. William Pelfrey, *The Big V* (New York: Liveright, 1972), p. 154.
7. Fussell, *Great War*, p. 35.
8. Ibid., p. ix.

3. Early Vietnam Writing, 1958–1970

1. Martin Russ, *Happy Hunting Ground* (New York: Atheneum, 1968), pp. 29–30; James Crumley, *One to Count Cadence* (New York: Random House, 1969), p. 283.
2. William Crawford Woods, *The Killing Zone* (New York: Harper's Magazine Press, 1970).
3. Robin Moore, *The Green Berets* (New York: Crown Publishers, 1965); Norman Mailer, *Why Are We in Vietnam?* (New York: G. P. Putnam's Sons, 1967).
4. Donald Duncan, *The New Legions* (New York: Random House, 1967).
5. Bernard Fall, *Last Reflections on a War* (Garden City, N.Y.: Doubleday, 1967), p. 28.
6. Alfred Kazin, *Bright Book of Life* (Boston: Little, Brown, 1973), p. 91.
7. William Faulkner, "The Bear," in *Big Woods* (New York: Random House, 1955), p. 13.
8. Gordon O. Taylor, "American Personal Narrative of the War in Vietnam," *American Literature* 52, no. 2 (May 1980): 294–308.
9. Asa Baber, *The Land of a Million Elephants* (New York:

William Morrow, 1970); John Sack, *M* (New York: New American Library, 1967); William Eastlake, *The Bamboo Bed* (New York: Simon & Schuster, 1969); Irwin R. Blacker, *Search and Destroy* (New York: Random House, 1966); John Briley, *The Traitors* (New York: G. P. Putnam's Sons, 1969); Victor Kolpacoff, *The Prisoners of Quai Dong* (New York: New American Library, 1967). The "metaphysical" character of its vision is described by Stanley Cooperman in "American War Novels: Yesterday, Today, and Tomorrow," *Yale Review* 61: 520.

10. Daniel Ford, *Incident at Muc Wa* (Garden City, N.Y.: Doubleday, 1967); Gene D. Moore, *The Killing at Ngo Tho* (New York: W. W. Norton, 1967); C. T. Morrison, *The Flame in the Icebox* (Jericho, N.Y.: Exposition Press, 1968); Tom Tiede, *Coward* (New York: Trident Press, 1968); John Rowe, *Count Your Dead* (Sydney: Angus & Robertson, 1968); Alan Clark, *The Lion Heart* (New York: William Morrow, 1969).

11. Richard Tregaskis, *Vietnam Diary* (New York: Holt, Rinehart & Winston, 1963); Ward Just, *To What End* (Boston: Houghton Mifflin, 1968). It might be added that since this early work, along with *Military Men*, mentioned earlier, Just has continued to write about Vietnam in a variety of modes. This work has included short fiction in collections such as *The Congressman Who Loved Flaubert and Other Stories* (Boston: Little, Brown, 1973), and *Honor, Power, Riches, Fame, and the Love of Women* (New York: E. P. Dutton, 1979), and a novel about a memory-haunted U.S. counterguerrilla operative entitled *Stringer* (Boston: Little, Brown, 1974).

12. Charles Coe, *Young Man in Vietnam* (New York: Four Winds Press, 1968); Larry Hughes, *You Can See a Lot*

Standing under a Flare in the Republic of Vietnam (New York: William Morrow, 1969); David Parks, *G.I. Diary* (New York: Harper & Row, 1965); Samuel Vance, *The Courageous and the Proud* (New York: W. W. Norton, 1970); David Douglas Duncan, *War without Heroes* (New York: Harper & Row, 1970).

13. Herman Melville, *The Confidence-Man* (New York: New American Library, 1964), p. 260.

14. In a kind of surreal updating of traditional war reportage, each of these is offered in specific association with an individual American soldier, whose full name is given as well as his home town. As an attempt to merge the possibilities of fact and fiction, this works to especially telling effect in the magazine format. See "M," *Esquire* 66, no. 4 (October 1966): 79–86, 140–62; and "When Demirgian Comes Marching Home Again, Hurrah? Hurrah?," *Esquire* 69, no. 1 (January 1968): 56–59, 124–27.

15. Frank Kermode, *The Sense of an Ending* (New York: Oxford University Press, 1967), p. 39.

16. Alexis de Tocqueville, *Democracy in America* (Garden City, N.Y.: Anchor Books, 1969), p. 488. The "prophecy" alluded to is his classic description of the national character, rendered after extensive travel and study in America during the 1830s: "Each citizen of a democracy generally spends his time considering the interests of a very insignificant person, namely himself. If he ever does raise his eyes higher, he sees nothing but the huge apparition of society or the even larger form of the human race. He has nothing between very limited and clear ideas and very general and vague conceptions; the space between is empty."

17. A recent writer has developed specific analogies between Vietnam narrative and "the new journalism." See John

Hellman, "The New Journalism and Vietnam: Memory and Structure in Michael Herr's *Dispatches*," *South Atlantic Quarterly* 79, no. 2 (Spring 1980): 141–51. Although I agree with much of what Hellman says, I find my own term more generally serviceable.

18. Norman Mailer, *The Executioner's Song* (Boston: Little, Brown, 1979).

19. William Styron, *Sophie's Choice* (New York: Random House, 1979).

20. Gloria Emerson, *Winners and Losers* (New York: Random House, 1976).

21. Arthur Kopit, *Indians* (New York: Hill & Wang, 1969).

22. D. H. Lawrence, *Studies in Classic American Literature* (New York: Viking Press, 1971), p. 30.

23. Ron Cowen, *Summertree* (New York: Random House, 1968); John Guare, *Cop-Out, Muzeeka, Home Fires: Three Plays* (New York: Grove Press, 1971).

24. See Robert Asahina, "The Basic Training of American Playwrights: Theater and the Vietnam War," *Theater* 9, no. 2: 30–37.

25. Robert B. Shaw, "The Poetry of Protest," in *American Poetry since 1960* (Cheadle, Cheshire, U.K.: Carcanet Press, 1973), pp. 45–54. For a more extended view of the topic, see also James B. Mersmann, *Out of the Vietnam Vortex* (Lawrence: University Press of Kansas, 1974).

26. Robert Bly, "The Teeth Mother Naked at Last," in *Sleepers Joining Hands* (New York: Harper & Row, 1973), pp. 18–26.

27. Walter Lowenfels, ed., *Where Is Vietnam?* (Garden City, N.Y.: Doubleday, Anchor Books, 1967).

28. Larry Rottmann, ed., *Winning Hearts and Minds: Poems by Vietnam Veterans* (New York: McGraw-Hill, 1972);

Michael Casey, *Obscenities* (New Haven, Conn.: Yale University Press, 1972).

29. Samuel Langhorne Clemens [Mark Twain], *The Adventures of Huckleberry Finn* (New York: W. W. Norton, 1977), p. 20.

30. Stephen Crane, *The Red Badge of Courage* (New York: W. W. Norton, 1976), p. 50.

31. John Balaban, *After Our War* (Pittsburgh: University of Pittsburgh Press, 1974); Bruce Weigl, *A Romance* (Pittsburgh: University of Pittsburgh Press, 1979).

32. Kermode, *Sense of an Ending*, p. 133.

4. In the Middle Range, 1970–1975

1. James Park Sloan, *War Games* (Boston: Houghton Mifflin, 1971); Josiah Bunting, *The Lionheads* (New York: George Braziller, 1972); Robert Roth, *Sand in the Wind* (Boston: Little, Brown, 1973); William Turner Huggett, *Body Count* (New York: G. P. Putnam's Sons, 1973); Tom Mayer, *Weary Falcon* (Boston: Houghton Mifflin, 1971); Wayne Karlin, Basil T. Paquet, and Larry Rottmann, eds., *Free Fire Zone* (New York: McGraw-Hill/First Casualty Press, 1973).

2. Joe Haldeman, *War Year* (New York: Holt, Rinehart & Winston, 1972). Other works of memoir from the period include Edward G. Briscoe, *Diary of a Short-Timer in Vietnam* (New York: Vantage Press, 1970); Edward Bernard, *Going Home* (Philadelphia: Dorrance, 1973); and John L. Cook, *The Advisor* (Philadelphia: Dorrance, 1973). See also pertinent sections of Anthony B. Herbert, *Soldier* (New York: Holt, Rinehart & Winston, 1973); and William

C. Westmoreland, *A Soldier Reports* (Garden City, N.Y.: Doubleday, 1976). There also continued to be considerable production of documentary narrative. See James Willwerth, *Eye in the Last Storm* (New York: Grossman Publishers, 1972); James Jones, *Viet Journal* (New York: Delacorte Press, 1973); and Donald Kirk, *Tell It to the Dead* (Chicago: Nelson-Hall, 1975).

3. Tim O'Brien, *If I Die in a Combat Zone* (New York: Delacorte Press, 1973). Quoted material in the text is from a more recent edition (New York: Dell, 1979) that includes some final revisions.

4. Frances Fitzgerald, *Fire in the Lake* (Boston: Little, Brown, 1972).

5. Robert Jay Lifton, *Home from the War* (New York: Simon & Schuster, 1973); Robert Stone, *Dog Soldiers* (Boston: Houghton Mifflin, 1974).

6. These works are described in some detail by Asahina in the article on Vietnam drama cited earlier.

7. H. Wesley Balk, *The Dramatization of 365 Days* (Minneapolis: University of Minnesota Press, 1972); David Rabe, *The Basic Training of Pavlo Hummel* and *Sticks and Bones* (New York: Viking Press, 1973), and *Streamers* (New York: Alfred A. Knopf, 1977).

8. Jan Berry and W. D. Ehrhart, eds., *Demilitarized Zones: Veterans after Vietnam* (Perkasie, Pa.: East River Anthology, 1976); D. C. Berry, *Saigon Cemetery* (Athens: University of Georgia Press, 1972).

9. I should note even as I begin this section that I hardly mean it to be a negative critique of metafictionist strategies in general. Like John Barth, in "The Literature of Replenishment," *Atlantic* 245, no. 1 (January 1981): 65–71, I find in the best postmodern fiction no evidence

of some requisite split between a highly developed conception of self-conscious artifice and a sense of the
fullness and immediacy of life as it is actually lived. Indeed, like the work of postmodern masters such as
Marquez, Kundera, and Calvino, the strongest Vietnam
metafiction—and *War Games* is an early example of considerable merit—makes its most significant meanings
precisely to the degree that these categories of vision become creatively interfused.

10. As in the film *Apocalypse Now*, with one of the things it
did get stunningly right, this might be best thought of in
terms of "The End" as done voice-over by Jim Morrison.

11. What Pound in particular actually called "Kulchur."

12. Joan Didion, *The White Album* (New York: Simon &
Schuster, 1979), p. 11.

5. The New Literature of Vietnam, 1975 to the Present

1. C. D. B. Bryan, *Friendly Fire* (New York: G. P. Putnam's
Sons, 1976); Ron Kovic, *Born on the Fourth of July* (New
York: McGraw-Hill, 1976); Winston Groom, *Better Times
Than These* (New York: Summit Books, 1978); James
Webb, *Fields of Fire* (Englewood Cliffs, N.J.: Prentice-Hall,
1978). One further novel of recent years, about CIA clan-
destine operations, is John Cassidy's *A Station in the
Delta* (New York: Charles Scribner's Sons, 1979).

2. See Hellman, "The New Journalism and Vietnam,"
pp. 142–43. For a recent attempt at a modal approach,
quite similar to Hellmann's and my own, that links *Dispatches* profitably with Caputo's *A Rumor of War* and

Kovic's *Born on the Fourth of July*, see also Peter McInerny, "'Straight' and 'Secret' History in Vietnam War Literature," *Contemporary Literature* 22, no. 2 (Spring 1981): 187–204.

3. Melville, *Moby Dick*, p. 88.

4. Herman Melville, *Billy Budd* (Chicago: University of Chicago Press, 1962), p. 128.

5. A third recent autobiographical work, more properly described as a journal rather than a memoir, is Frederick Downs, *The Killing Zone* (New York: W. W. Norton, 1978).

6. In itself, this sort of "going beyond," considered in historical perspective, does not seem to have been peculiar to Vietnam. James Jones observes, for instance, in one of the "Evolution of a Soldier" sections of *WW II*, that a common final step in the process was the combatant's simple acceptance of the inevitability of his own death. At the far end of experience in battle, he writes, there could come "the ultimate luxury of just *not giving a damn* anymore." See *WW II* (New York: Grosset & Dunlap, 1975), pp. 38, 54. What would seem to distinguish the idea in this case, and also in similar ones that present themselves in a number of other narratives from Vietnam, is the sense of utter futility with which it is attended.

7. In reflecting on the legal resolution of Caputo's case, one cannot help recalling also the scene in *Catch-22* where MPs, breaking into a room where Aarfy has just thrown a young girl to her death on the street several stories below, ignore him and instead arrest Yossarian, who has just walked into the room, for being in Rome without a pass. See the chapter entitled "The Eternal City," *Catch-22* (New York: Simon & Schuster, 1961), pp. 396–410.

8. This is the recapitulation of an insight that supplies the focal idea for a novel mentioned earlier, Victor Kolpacoff's *The Prisoners of Quai Dong;* and as I shall note presently, a variation on the same image emerges in one of the fantasy sections of *Going after Cacciato,* where a Viet Cong officer tells his American adversaries, "We are prisoners, all of us. POWs" (p. 96).

9. It is an expression Melville uses in both *Moby-Dick* and *Billy Budd* to characterize his concept of microcosm.

10. Some of these, one may recall, are word-for-word the same lessons with which *If I Die in a Combat Zone* concludes (pp. 198–99). Here, for the experimental novelist, they provide a kind of new beginning.

11. I have mentioned the similarity of O'Brien's view of literary sense-making to that characteristic of what has been called "magical realism." A more general version of that analogy would seem to hold true for a good deal of recent Vietnam writing. Increasingly it suggests a conscious inquiry into the processes of an art capable, often for all its seeming "unreality," of indeed transforming reality into something somehow truer than it ever was in experiential fact.

6. Conclusion

1. Charles Coleman, *Sergeant Back Again* (New York: Harper & Row, 1980).

2. Al Santoli, *Everything We Had* (New York: Random House, 1981); Mark Baker, *Nam* (New York: William Morrow, 1981).

3. See for instance a review by Peter S. Prescott in *News-*

week, January 19, 1981, pp. 82, 84, and also anonymous notices in *Kirkus Reviews*, October 1, 1980, pp. 1309–10, and *Publishers Weekly*, October 24, 1980, p. 34.

4. See again Peter S. Prescott, *Newsweek*, May 4, 1981, pp. 78, 80. See also R. Z. Sheppard's commentary in *Time*, April 20, 1981, pp. 88, 90; Mark Leepson's in the *New York Times Book Review*, May 17, 1981, p. 12; and Frances Fitzgerald's in *New Boston Review*, May–June 1981, pp. 10–11.

5. William Manchester, *Good-Bye Darkness* (Boston: Little, Brown, 1980).

Index

Index

Index

Index